Minding the Achievement Gap

One Classroom at a Time

SUSTAINABLE
FORESTRY
INITIATIVE

Certified Fiber Sourcing

www.sfiprogram.org

JANE E. POLLOCK   SHARON M. FORD
MARGARET M. BLACK

the curriculum

the plan book

the gradebook

Minding the
Achievement
Gap

One
Classroom
at a Time

ASCD
Alexandria, Virginia USA

ASCD®

1703 N. Beauregard St. • Alexandria, VA 22311-1714 USA
Phone: 800-933-2723 or 703-578-9600 • Fax: 703-575-5400
Website: www.ascd.org • E-mail: member@ascd.org
Author guidelines: www.ascd.org/write

Gene R. Carter, *Executive Director;* Ed Milliken, *Chief Program Officer;* Carole Hayward, *Publisher;*
Laura Lawson, *Acquisitions Editor;* Julie Houtz, *Director, Book Editing & Production;* Katie Martin, *Editor;*
Georgia Park, *Senior Graphic Designer;* Mike Kalyan, *Production Manager;* Cynthia Stock, *Typesetter;*
Kyle Steichen, *Production Specialist*

All web links in this book are correct as of the publication date below but may have become inactive or
otherwise modified since that time. If you notice a deactivated or changed link, please e-mail books@
ascd.org with the words "Link Update" in the subject line. In your message, please specify the web link,
the book title, and the page number on which the link appears.

PAPERBACK ISBN: 978-1-4166-1384-8   ASCD product #112005   n5/12
Also available as an e-book (see Books in Print for the ISBNs).

Quantity discounts for the paperback edition only: 10–49 copies, 10%; 50+ copies, 15%; for 1,000 or
more copies, call 800-933-2723, ext. 5634, or 703-575-5634. For desk copies: member@ascd.org.

Library of Congress Cataloging-in-Publication Data

Pollock, Jane E., 1958–
    Minding the achievement gap one classroom at a time / Jane E. Pollock, Sharon M. Ford,
Margaret M. Black.
        p. cm.
    Includes bibliographical references and index.
    ISBN 978-1-4166-1384-8 (pbk. : alk. paper)
    1. Educational equalization—United States. 2. Academic achievement—United States. I. Ford,
Sharon M. II. Black, Margaret M. III. Title.
    LC213.2.P65 2012
    379.2'60973—dc23
                                        2012000469

22 21 20 19 18 17 16 15 14 13 12   1 2 3 4 5 6 7 8 9 10 11 12

To Barry.
—JEP

To Gary, and to my mother, Doris.
—SMF

With gratefulness to Governor T. G. Thompson,
who believed a stay-at-home had a contribution to make,
and to my sister, Sue, with whom I make "Black, party of two."
—MMB

Minding the Achievement Gap
One Classroom at a Time

Introduction

JILL CULLIS, A HIGH SCHOOL GOVERNMENT TEACHER WITH 20 YEARS of experience, remembers her epiphany clearly.

"I am told there is a moment in every person's career that forever changes the perception each of us has about what we've done in the past and what we can accomplish in the future," she says. "For me, that moment took place the day that Andrew Romanoff, then the Speaker of the House in the Colorado legislature, came to my class to talk with my students."

Jill describes her school community near Denver, Colorado, as "disadvantaged urban." She had been told that during Speaker Romanoff's visit, he would be discussing new opportunities for high school students and the critical importance of finishing high school. He said he sought to have an "honest conversation," and Jill knew he would certainly get *that* from her students.

Because Speaker Romanoff was not the first politician guest speaker to visit the class, Jill expected him to offer newly packaged nostrums involving technology, flexible schedules, and maybe scholarships to attend college. Fairly confident, Jill waited for her students to tell the Speaker what they always told her: they were typical teenagers who lacked personal motivation, their parents were too busy to participate in or support school events, and the state incentives would only interest the students who were likely to graduate anyway. But instead of offering platitudes tied to scholarships, Speaker Romanoff had an announcement and a question. "We are working at the state level to intentionally close the achievement gap, especially for students in schools like yours—with lower achievement and potentially high dropout rates," he said. "So what I want to ask you is this: What makes students drop out? What makes students drop out here, at your school?"

Darien spoke out first. "School is boring," he said. "*That's* what makes students drop out. If you want us to stay in school, then the teachers have to change how they teach us. You come to class and the teacher talks or maybe gives you a test. Sometimes you know how well you are doing, but sometimes it is just a big surprise at the end of the semester."

"I have to agree," Alicia said. "We come to school, but some of our teachers—I don't want to say this, but they seem to get excited only if they can take points away from us. Sometimes there are students who just don't do anything in class, and the teacher tells them 'they have a choice,' meaning that they are choosing not to work. I don't think those kids know how to do the assignments. Sometimes the teachers tell them they should have learned it before, but they didn't. After a while, the teacher just moves on ahead, leaving them behind, and that is just the way it is."

Raul spoke up a bit timidly, saying, "I also think that some teachers are happy as long as we give the right answers or stay quiet. Sometimes I do have something to say, but I don't get the chance, so I just sit quietly."

For Jill Cullis, *this* was the moment that changed everything.

"Until then," Jill says, "I had been proud of consecutive years of 'Exceeds Expectations' in my evaluations and my two Teacher of the Year awards. But when I heard what my students had to say about class, knowing they could very well have been describing me on some days, I admitted to myself that I was the only person responsible for planning and delivering the instruction in my class-room, and that maybe I had been abdicating my responsibility to teach better.

"Please understand that I am not of the opinion that instruction needs to compete with the latest video game, but I knew that I, too, had students earning Ds and Fs, and saw some of my students looking bored during my instruction, and I had heard myself say those phrases before, like, 'You should already know how to take notes.' I realized that even though I did plan lessons and teach every day, it had not occurred to me that I should have intentionally worked to close the achievement gap every day in every class. Most of the students in my classes are academically at risk because of language or low income, but I truly believe that it took that moment, listening to my own students, to realize that I needed to do something about achievement without a reform, without an initiative, but simply by changing my own planning and delivery. I just had to find the right tools."

The persistent presence of underachieving students, students who graduate from high school ill-prepared for college and the workplace, and students who do not graduate at all confirms that we must continue to find new solutions. While politicians secure taxpayer support and funding for these efforts, and policymakers seek ways to reinvent and redesign schooling for the globally oriented 21st century, teachers can apply current research and use practical techniques to help academically at-risk students make vital progress.

Today's research shows that what works in schools to advance student achievement is intentional teaching. Stated more directly, most education reform funding and attention is directed toward improving education by changing school factors, such as structures, schedules, and curriculum materials. However, as we will see in this book, it is the teacher effect—demonstrated through instructional planning and actual teaching and assessment practices in the classroom—that is the single most powerful measure influencing student learning in schools today. It is within every teacher's reach to be a great teacher, rather than just a good teacher, and to close the achievement gap for academically at-risk students one classroom at a time. To do so, however, teachers will need to reexamine and adjust their teaching and assessment habits. Like Jill explained, being willing to take responsibility and then action means finding out about and applying research about what works.

This book is the fourth in an unofficial series aimed at improving student learning that began with *Classroom Instruction That Works* (Marzano, Pickering, & Pollock, 2001) and its look at nine instructional strategies shown by research to raise student achievement. Five years after coauthoring *Classroom Instruction That Works,* Jane E. Pollock ("Janie" to friends and in these pages) concluded that although teachers and administrators were reading about the nine high-yield strategies, discussing them in book studies, and focusing on them for staff development, this familiarity with the strategies was not translating into widespread student learning gains. The problem, it seemed to Janie, was that teachers learned about the strategies but did not deliberately adjust their teaching habits to incorporate the strategies; more important, teachers failed to recognize that the high-yield strategies were techniques students needed to learn, and that teachers needed to teach students how to use the strategies every day in every class.

In 2007, Janie addressed this issue when she wrote *Improving Student Learning One Teacher at a Time,* a book that introduced a lesson-planning schema known as GANAG. An update of Madeline C. Hunter's Mastery Teaching schema published in the 1970s, the GANAG schema guides teachers to intentionally incorporate the nine strategies into daily classroom learning activities. Two years later, Janie and Sharon M. Ford wrote *Improving Student Learning One Principal at a Time* (Pollock & Ford, 2009), which focused on how principals and instructional coaches could use GANAG in supervision to provide more useful feedback to teachers about how to effectively incorporate high-yield strategies in preparation and delivery of instruction. Janie and Sharon have worked with individual teachers as well as school and district administrators who are eager to share about the gains they have made by following the approaches presented in these two books—how (usually over the course of a single school year) they have raised test scores, met adequate yearly progress (AYP) goals, and raised ACT scores, and how they have sustained these gains in following years.

A few years ago, Margaret M. Black ("Peggy") suggested that Janie adapt GANAG to increase engagement and achievement for English language learners (ELLs), students with learning disabilities, and other academically at-risk learners. When specialists working in pull-out resource rooms and inclusion classrooms used GANAG, students showed gains in achievement, and teachers improved communication among themselves and with students and parents. It confirmed what each of us—Janie, Sharon, and Peggy—had believed: the GANAG schema had the potential to help any teacher reach any student and, in effect, close the achievement gap on a classroom-by-classroom basis.

Minding the Achievement Gap One Classroom at a Time offers both classroom teachers and specialists guidance based on research and practice that works for all ages, all curriculum areas, and all student populations, but is especially effective in helping academically at-risk students, including students who are English language learners and who receive special education services. The approaches we share involve teachers intentionally changing their teaching habits to (1) deliberately provide learning goals; (2) teach students to interact with these goals by tracking their own progress; and (3) purposefully use and direct students to use high-yield learning strategies that maximize feedback as a way to further all students' engagement. Based on research and the successes we have seen, we believe such changes in teaching practices can raise achievement and develop more self-regulated and better-prepared students.

We begin in Chapter 1 by pointing out that neither the achievement gap nor efforts to close it are new developments. The purpose of this discussion is to demystify reform efforts and sensationalized educational crises. Efforts to raise achievement levels of *all* children in the United States stretch back hundreds of years, and many of these reforms have appropriately focused on school structures. Using recent research that testifies that the most effective way to improve student achievement is to shift reform attention away from structural school factors toward the classroom, we emphasize the importance of teachers reexamining their instructional planning and assessment practices in order to help all students raise achievement every day in every class.

Chapter 2 discusses how tools easily available to every teacher—curriculum documents, a plan book, and a grade book—can be coordinated through GANAG to boost student learning. We discuss ways that teachers can exponentially increase the effectiveness of feedback by revising their usual planning and delivery habits. The design of GANAG cues students to use high-yield strategies to reach specific curriculum goals—both lesson content and lesson skills—and GANAG gives teachers an intentional way to connect the curriculum to their plan book and their grade book.

Chapter 3 addresses academically at-risk students who don't "do school" well and appear unmotivated. We propose a solution to increase engagement and promote master learning: the use of interactive notebooks in concert with the phases of GANAG and the nine high-yield strategies. The "interactive" quality of the notebook redefines how feedback can change the engagement of otherwise passive learners.

In Chapter 4, we take a closer look at English language learners, a critical subgroup of academically at-risk students. ELLs constitute a growing population of children in U.S. schools. This chapter deliberately addresses the "Gs" of GANAG—goal setting and goal review —in both the planning and delivery of instruction. We point out that English language learning standards are available in every state, and teachers can use them intentionally as the learning objective rather than as just a checklist to assess students. Adapting GANAG to include both content and language goals allows EL specialists and general education teachers to deliberately monitor student progress toward both language acquisition and content goals during pull-out or inclusion classroom time.

Chapter 5 discusses GANAG for special education teachers and introduces an adaptation called GANAGPlus that increases and improves communication and instructional coordination between co-teachers. Blending co-teaching methods with the phases of GANAG allows for synchronized teaching and assessment. In addition, any student in a pull-out or resource classroom also benefits when the teacher organizes his or her lessons to intentionally provide instruction and frequent feedback toward progress on curriculum goals, which are the underlying steps of the GANAG schema.

We appreciate the efforts made by all educators to mind the achievement gap and are especially grateful to those who have provided the "Educator Voices" between the chapters of this book. Often classroom teachers and specialists can "say it best" in their own words, and here they do, sharing experiences about how concepts we present are working in real classrooms and schools. The insight they provide is a valuable part of the conversation.

All educators who read this book should be able to reaffirm their belief in the power a teacher has to improve student learning. We know that every teacher can actively mind and close the achievement gap, one classroom at a time.

1

Minding the Achievement Gap

"CLOSING ACHIEVEMENT GAPS IS MORE URGENT TODAY THAN EVER before, and dramatic success is possible. Academic excellence is difficult to achieve, but is not a controversial goal," writes economist Ronald Ferguson in *Toward Excellence with Equity* (2008, p. 284). Countless agencies produce vast amounts of literature focused on the notable disparity that exists between the educational achievement of white and minority students (primarily black and Hispanic). Much of this literature shares Ferguson's sentiment that closing the achievement gap is an urgent national imperative. We think it is, too.

We agree with Ferguson that group-proportional racial equality in achievement is an important goal for the nation, but we are mindful that significant learning gaps exist for other populations of students, too, including those who are living in situational or generational poverty, those who are not proficient in English, and those who have disabilities and receive special education services. We further agree that making it possible for every student in the United States to achieve academic success is an uncontroversial goal—and a compelling one for every educator in every classroom, every day.

Centuries of Schools in Crisis

As urgent a priority as closing achievement gaps seems today, the penchant to propose broad educational reform to close the educational achievement gap has been around for a very long time. The Massachusetts Education Law of

7

1642, for example, required that parents or guardians see to it that their children could read and write (in order to follow the laws and know the principles of their religion). This was less a reflection of the value that colonists placed on schooling than it was recognition that surviving in the New World required certain sets of skills and knowledge. The Law of 1647 later required towns with 50 families or more to build a school and hire a schoolmaster to teach children to read and write. In just five years, the colonists realized that there was an achievement gap and that the solution was to create schools for all children in the town to attend.

Another example, 200 years later, reveals another achievement gap. In 1845, the results of the first standardized test administered to 500 students in Boston distressed Horace Mann, secretary of the Massachusetts State Board of Education, who concluded, "What little students knew came from memorizing the textbook without having to think about the meaning of what they had learned" (Rothstein, 1998, p. 17). Mann proposed a way to close the learning gap he saw: improve teacher preparation so that all students had access to schools with highly qualified instructors.

In *The Way We Were? The Myths and Realities of America's Student Achievement*, Richard Rothstein (1998) covers 100 years of U.S. school reform efforts aimed at tackling "educational crises" like the one Mann noted. Many of these crises seem strikingly contemporary to a modern reader—from poor literacy in New York during the Great Depression, to inadequate knowledge of world geography in the 1940s, deficient understanding of mathematics in the 1960s, subpar critical thinking skills in the 1970s, and a lack of workplace skills in the 1980s, all the way up the present-day perception that students do not have the 21st century skills they will need in a global, knowledge-based economy.

Some of the recent explorations of key gaps in the educational attainment of U.S. students include *Democracy at Risk* (Forum for Education and Democracy, 2008) and *A Stagnant Nation: Why American Students Are Still at Risk* (Strong American Schools, 2008). We suspect if Rothstein were asked to comment on the urgency insinuated by new reports describing achievement gaps, he might quote Will Rogers, as he did in his 1998 book, saying, "The schools ain't what they used to be and probably never were" (p. 17).

Time to Reflect

How does knowing that rhetoric about "educational crises" dates back to the colonial era affect your perspective on the current achievement gap?

Unnecessarily Ambitious Reforms

Rothstein's research touches on two particularly noteworthy issues. First, he affirms that evidence repeatedly shows achievement levels in the United States to be better than they have been in years past, but he adds that good news does not necessarily make for good news stories. Second, Rothstein expresses apprehension about what he refers to as political "hyperventilated rhetoric." He contends that repeated speech making about the dire state of U.S. education leads to the crafting of unnecessarily ambitious education reforms rather than to the implementation of thoughtful, effective plans. Because the populace believes schools are performing so unsatisfactorily—so much more poorly than "they used to"—educators and politicians are designing broad reforms that look very different from targeted reform aimed at making generally satisfactory schools better and helping those students who really are at risk of academic failure. Rothstein goes on to quip, almost apologetically, that people who pay to fund schools might need to perceive a situation as a crisis before they are willing to act.

Empiricist Gene Glass, best known for originating the concept of meta-analysis in the fields of psychology and education, is careful to point out that *schools in crisis* is a not a new concept: "Criticism and reform of the education of young people was old when Quintilian (35–95 A.D.) was young" (2008, p. 4). Glass argues that inflated impressions of a crisis in education can have detrimental consequences, influencing choices for reform initiatives at the national level that trickle down to guide local decisions and budget expenditures.

When we read commentary about schools today not performing "well enough," there is often an implication and sometimes even a direct assertion that subpar schools put national prosperity at risk. Both Glass and Rothstein argue that the relationship between education and the economy is far more complicated than the simple picture painted by school critics. More critically, they point out that myths about school failure can lead to ill-conceived reform measures that set up the public to conclude that the public school system is irretrievably broken and cannot be fixed.

From Rhetoric to Targeted Change

It is important for educators to reaffirm that closing the achievement gap is not a recent effort in the United States; it is more accurately seen as an ongoing challenge—one that is now our turn to tackle, with both the wisdom of historical perspective and the scientific insight of research informing our approach. As we seize this opportunity, we must remember that exaggerated rhetoric leads to wide political or radical reform action that tends to burn out before the next political reform. When it comes to achieving significant, long-term learning improvement for students, smaller, more targeted changes are what work best, and teachers can play a vital part in those changes every day (Marzano et al., 2001).

❈ Time to Reflect ❈

In what ways does the current narrative about the achievement gap at the national level affect local school decisions about the steps to take to improve student learning?

Mind the Gap to Close the Gap

The pithy phrase "mind the gap" has been popularized by the London Underground railway to help passengers heed the uneven space between the subway door and the station platform. Although engineers tested various solutions (such as rebuilding and adding bridges), they decided the best course of action was to teach passengers to automatically step across the breach. So there are billboards and robotic voices that admonish commuters to "mind the gap." Having learned to do so, commuters carry on with their daily business, and there is no need to look to engineers to perform a massive and costly transformation.

When it comes to improving education, although the difference between "closing" the gap and "minding" it may seem inconsequential, the terminology represents a critical change in perspective—encouraging empowered educators to make subtle changes in their work rather than wait for communication about broad-based, top-down initiatives that may have little to do with the reality that they see. "Closing the gap," in addition, seems unintentionally negative and generally admonishes the school or district to "fix" what may be low achievement "created or caused" by the school. "Minding the gap," on the other hand, suggests attentiveness and thoughtful action.

Teachers Can Change the Valence

Sometime shortly after being sworn in as president in 1801, Thomas Jefferson wrote to scientist Joseph Priestley about various possibilities of "innovation." In a biography about Priestley, Stephen Johnson (2008) notes that in the 1800s, "innovation" was a negative term, because new development was seen as detrimental to the existing order. Jefferson and Priestley, however, used the term to mean "a looking forward, not backward, for improvement." The negative connotation of "innovation" was transformed to a positive. As Johnson puts it, "The change of valence of the word [innovation] over the next century is one measure of society's shifting relationship to progress" (p. 198).

In this book, we present information and ideas that we hope will inspire educators to change the valence of the word "gap." If teachers consider an achievement gap as an opportunity to make an improvement, then they will find ways to shift the progress of improving learning for all students.

Teachers can mind the gap they see in their classrooms. They can, with self-initiative and without delay, adjust their instructional and assessment practices rather than wait a year for the next data retreat or until the end-of-term or end-of-year test results confirm that learning gaps exist. Most school-based efforts undertaken explicitly to "close the gap" focus on analyzing summative test results from annual external measures and making generalized judgments on the status of population groups. Because the scores typically come late in the school year and long after the tests are actually administered, data analysis about the actual scores themselves is generally the most we can do at that point in time—a reality that leaves many administrators and teachers feeling power-less because the students have moved on to another grade level and the data usually confirm what was already known. This is why educators face the arrival of test scores with a certain fatalism.

Many educators know that once external test scores arrive, it is too late in the school year to help specific students who have fallen short of learning goals make the gains they need in order to catch up. In contrast, teachers who mind the gap in their own classrooms know which students are not performing well and can adjust their practices accordingly, making intentional instruction and formative assessment decisions that improve both lesson planning and daily teaching. Minding the gap suggests action that is taken during instruction to support and keep students from falling into a pattern of low achievement or disengagement. Effective teaching, with ongoing adjustments for student learning throughout the year, allows teachers to continue moving forward with academically at-risk students.

⚒ Time to Reflect ⚒

What are the advantages to changing the conversation from "closing" the gap to intentionally and voluntarily "minding" the gap?

Effective Schools

Most teachers will admit that there are students in their classes who could perform better. Some of these "academically at-risk" students have disabilities or emerging language skills, while others may be described as unmotivated—derailed by boredom or by a lack of background knowledge that makes learning obstacles seem insurmountable. Having students who persistently fall short of the pre-scribed learning outcomes contributes to teacher frustration, which is only com-pounded when these teachers continue to use strategies that do not get results rather than investigate new practices that might increase student achievement.

The Effective Schools movement of the 1970s launched an admirable charge to improve learning led by teachers and administrators within the profession. Many "best practices in teaching" lists emerged during this time, most advocating increased student involvement in learning guided by teachers engaged in some form of professional development that encouraged collabora-tion and reflective self-evaluation of teaching effectiveness. Education profes-sionals have since built on this foundation, incorporating many of these best practices into more recent efforts to focus student learning on curriculum goals and use instructional strategies proven to bring gains in student learning.

More recently, Steven Covey (1989) has written extensively about the habits of successful people, and one tenet that applies here is a tactic he calls "sharpening the saw." In one anecdote Covey shares, a person saws a load of wood using a dull saw. Another person who has been observing the labori-ous task suggests that the first person should "sharpen the saw." But the first person declines, contending that "If I stop to sharpen the saw, I won't get the work done." Covey recommends that each of us find a way to "sharpen the saw" in our own lives or professions, because it is a way to renew, preserve, and enhance oneself. One simple way for teachers to sharpen their pedagogical saws is to look to research, which reveals that what works in schools to advance student achievement is intentional teaching, dependent on teachers' willing-ness to reexamine planning methods, instructional practices, and assessment habits in order to determine how to help all students make gains, especially those characterized as academically at risk or underachieving.

The Power of the Teacher Effect

According to John Hattie (2009), author of *Visible Learning: A Synthesis of Over 800 Meta-analyses Relating to Achievement,* many national reforms advocated as ways to close the achievement gap (e.g., reducing class size, offering out-of-school curricula, providing more scheduled time for teachers to meet) are worthy innovations. But, he points out, the research repeatedly shows that reforms like these, focused on school and schedule structures, do not lead to significant student achievement gains. The effort invested in implementing structural adaptations would be better invested in Covey's "saw sharpening"— in teachers improving the ways in which they make the learning goals and success criteria clear to the students, using direct instruction that includes high-yield strategies, and providing effective and frequent feedback to the learners. According to Hattie, it is the *teacher* effect on student achievement that education reform efforts ought to focus on, not the school effect.

In his compendium of studies related to student achievement from 1995 to the present, Hattie (2009) observes that many teachers do sincerely try to use new techniques every year, but that "research concluded that any typical innovation a teacher uses can be expected to change average affective and achievement outcomes by 0.2 and 0.4 standard deviations" (p. 12), which Hattie deems between a small- and a medium-sized gain.

What this means is that teachers have been introducing new strategies for years (which is good), but most new techniques result in only nominal gains; those interventions need to be able to compete with the powerful effect that out-of-school factors (home influences, resources, demographic characteristics) have on low-performing students or marginalized populations. What's more, when teachers who do try a new approach find, at the end of the school year, that their low-performing groups have not made the hoped-for gains in test scores or grades, these teachers tend to drop the strategy and introduce a new one the following year.

Many educators have experienced a similar large-scale "bandwagon" approach in which every teacher in the school or a district is expected to implement one strategy to increase student achievement in a marginalized population. When the end-of-the-year test scores do not indicate gains, everyone collectively tries another new strategy. The result, as many teachers have told us, is "initiative fatigue" combined with the disappointing fact that their pedagogical efforts produced no significant student achievement gains.

Hattie's research corroborates the contention that shifting attention from the school to the individual classroom teacher is the key to lasting and significant changes in achievement. When a teacher deliberately seeks and implements innovations that incorporate high-yield strategies (those boosting outcomes by 0.4 or more standard deviations), students with marginalized achievement levels will show proficiency gains that trump negative out-of-school factors (p. 9). This conclusion underscores points made earlier in this chapter: shifting improvement efforts from the school to the classroom and changing automatic teaching habits, including the ways daily lessons are prepared and delivered, are imperative. Teachers can sharpen their pedagogical saws by (1) improving the ways in which they make learning goals and success criteria clear to the students, (2) planning for and using direct instruction that includes high-yield strategies, and (3) providing effective and frequent feedback to the learners.

⚔ Time to Reflect ⚒

How could your school use Hattie's findings to improve student learning?

A Light That Has Dimmed

On Edweek's *Teacher Magazine*/Living in Dialogue blog, teacher-leader Anthony Cody (2009) shared this observation:

> According to test score data released today, California students have increased their ability to pass state tests so that fully half of them are proficient in English (up from 46 percent a year ago), and 46 percent are proficient in math (up from 43 percent a year ago).
>
> However, the achievement gap remains as wide as ever, with only 47 percent of African American and Latino students performing at a proficient level in English. This does not come as any shock to most educators. For all the emphasis on closing the gap, little has really changed for these students.
>
> One thing seems clear: Eight years of "shining a bright light" on the achievement gap seems to have made very little difference.

Anthony Cody is right to point out that years of "shining a light" on the achievement gap have done fairly little, so far, to close that gap. Schools embrace new school-improvement measures on a regular basis, yet, as indicated by research, innovations tend to be structural (e.g., addressing the schedules, working conditions, and extracurricular activities) and make very little impact on academic outcomes, especially for students who are academically at risk.

What this tells us is that educators need a different, brighter light. School and district leaders can support teachers best through initiatives to change individual teachers' pedagogical habits. Studies show that a teacher who seeks professional feedback about instructional practices can produce strong gains, even in classrooms with students who previously performed poorly (Pressley, Gaskins, Solic, & Collins, 2006). Teachers and principals who work in tandem to change automatic teaching habits see greater gains in student achievement (Pollock & Ford, 2009).

Each Teacher Holds the Key

We agree with Glass and Rothstein, who suggest that steadfast, minor changes made by teachers at the classroom level are the real key to long-term improvement in student learning. High school teacher Jill Cullis, whom we heard from in this book's Introduction, would probably agree as well. She asserts that the best thing that happened to her disadvantaged students was that after two decades of teaching, she decided to learn to teach better. Within a year of her "momentous epiphany," the achievement scores of students in her class had increased an average of 20 points.

"In the past," Jill says, "I could ignore the lofty goals we heard in meetings year after year about 'closing the gap' because they always sounded like mandates for administrators, whereas the tasks teachers were asked to accomplish in data retreats often simply confirmed that our students were not performing well. But we already knew that.

"Minding the gap the way I do now is unusual because I don't honestly think anyone really expects the classroom teacher to be the factor that closes the achievement gap; everyone assumes it takes a national or state reform effort.

But now I have the tools I need to attend to student achievement daily in my classroom. It's a matter of being much more mindful of student responses and perspectives, planning for and assessing changes in their learning, and teaching students how to assess their own learning."

Teachers are the most important factor in student success, but only if they deliberately use teaching practices to change students' low performances. In the next four chapters, we will take a closer look at specific techniques that all teachers can use to mind the gap within their existing classroom structures to help students of all abilities, regardless of the challenges they face, become more successful learners.

⚔ Time to Reflect ⚔

What can you do, as a teacher or an administrator, to mind the gap?

In some ways, we are at a crossroads in time in education; at this opportune point, we can use the knowledge of historical trends and perceived gaps in learning combined with the firm directions where research can point us in order to effectively educate *all* students. We have opportunities to make thoughtful decisions that will lead to targeted change in classrooms rather than attempting broad-based district and school reforms that may not promote student learning and close achievement gaps. Teachers have an essential role to play. By attentively focusing on improving classroom instruction and student learning outcomes, they can effectively mind, and thus close, achievement gaps.

Educator Voice

Kathy Gwidt, District Adminstrator

Part of Kathy Gwidt's job as Director of Teaching and Learning in the School District of New London in Wisconsin is to guide administrative teams through the classroom observation process. During that process, she and others listened to students describe their successes and how they fell short of achieving academically. Kathy and her colleagues now realize the power and value of common language and effective feedback. It has led them to effectively mind the gap by classroom, not by school.

"How Could This Happen?"

"Being the student I am, I never thought I would make it into advanced math."

When asked what he meant by this comment, Corey, a high school junior, explained that he was "not one of the smart kids." We knew that Corey had a 1.0 grade point average (GPA), but from the time of our introduction, I was struck by how little that label seemed to fit this articulate young man. He confidently shook my hand, eloquently conversed about his middle school years, and defined "the smart kids" as those who had their agenda books signed and who regularly participated in class. Corey also told me that back in his elementary days he had been extremely successful in advanced-level math, a class in which homework was not graded, but quizzes and tests were. Corey explained that he never did the homework for this class but had maintained an *A* anyway. "Dream come true, right?" he snickered.

Corey's voice is representative of academic underachievers whom we interviewed in an effort to increase overall achievement in our district by better understanding student perception of grades and report cards. I talked with Corey and high school juniors who were identified by their GPAs as either *academic achievers* (those with GPAs ranging from 3.5 to 4.0) or *academic underachievers* (those with GPAs below 1.0). Although much research exists about grading and reporting, literature addressing student perception on the topic of achievement was limited, and I was committed to adding student voices to the plethora of research already published.

What our efforts to understand student perspective on achievement taught us was that we educators have a tremendous opportunity to mitigate achievement differences, regardless of genetic or environmental factors—and the way to do that is by shifting our focus from "closing" achievement gaps to "minding" them at the classroom level, with each individual student.

Corey was what I would describe as an introspective underachiever. He was thoughtful, independent, and confident, but achievement in school was not his primary concern. He was not a disruptive student; in fact, he was reserved and rarely spoke during class. Teachers generally were frustrated with Corey, seeing his unwillingness to participate in class or complete homework as a puzzling lack of responsibility on his part.

During our interview, Corey became a voice and a solution instead of a cipher. He continued to tell the story of his school experience, returning back to his unlikely presence in elementary school advanced math. His teacher had explained to him that his assessment scores were the highest in the class. When I asked how he had felt when his teacher told him this, Corey replied, "I sort of felt like . . . see, I knew [that] I knew that stuff, and I sort of had hope that school would make sense to me. Other years, teachers would just give me bad grades, and that was it. I look back and know I tried a lot harder [in the advanced math class]."

Continuing, Corey shared that by midyear, other students and even other teachers did not think it was fair that he could pass the class without completing homework, which, although not graded, was still "required." In response to complaints, the decision was made to move Corey to a regular math class—one in which homework was both required and graded. This class involved Corey repeating a lot of content he had already mastered, but it added the responsibility of homework. Corey did his homework in this class, and the department eventually moved him back to his original advanced course. Upon his return to the class, however, Corey once again stopped doing homework, and within a short period, he found himself back in a regular math class.

Corey's take on this? "While I bounced back and forth [between classes], I failed to learn, or missed bits [and pieces of instruction] that went on in both classes. I feel that missing that has had a big impact on my life."

I was left wondering how much of the entire scenario of underachievement was a function of our school policies inadvertently contributing to Corey "falling through the cracks." By not doing his math assignments, he was deemed to be "not performing well," but at the same time, he *could* perform the math. The actions taken to "help" Corey didn't motivate him the way the school had intended, didn't support his knowledge or performance, and may have led, as he believes, to further detrimental consequences. How many other academically at-risk students were our habitual practices hurting more than helping?

"That's the Way We Have Always Done It"

I work with exceptional educators who are dedicated to improving student achievement. Most have spent their careers attempting to balance shifts in the educational pendulum. We embrace a philosophy of continuous improvement and can clearly point to data that indicate learning gaps exist. We have worked diligently to comply with state and federal mandates, and according to all reports, we have done so successfully. Yet we know there are academic underachievers who have been alienated from a system that, even though unintentionally, does not embrace them.

We understand the history of grading and reporting, as well as current practices in these areas, but little appears to have changed to accommodate student needs. Despite research that encourages change, we have continued to teach, grade, and report in much the same way that we were taught, graded, and reported on as high school students. As we look at Corey, and at other students with similar stories, we know we cannot wait for grades and end-of-year data to confirm that learning gaps exist. Instead, we must be willing to grasp the value of adjusting classroom practices that improve instruction and ultimately achievement. To effect this change, we understand that we must acknowledge links between student perceptions and the context of everyday practice to avoid patterns of low achievement or disengagement.

A Switch to Minding the Gap

Traditions of grading and reporting of grades have remained sacred in the history of American education, so it would not have been a surprise if the staff and administrative team had remained satisfied with initiatives such as report card revisions or a change in grading and reporting policy. We were not. We knew that we needed more than structural change to realize sustained improvement; we needed change in the instructional practices at the classroom level.

Our staff had been working to develop clear learning targets, and principals embraced the GANAG framework in an effort to apply a common language to feedback that was provided to teachers during observations. Yet these strategies seemed to be applied inconsistently. Although teachers may have been stating the goal at the start of their lesson, for example, they weren't always teaching to it. And although there had been an immense amount of training provided to teachers, there was still plenty of confusion over how high-yield strategies could consistently be applied in a lesson. Classroom observations indicated the application of the strategies was minimal.

This is when we realized that we, the administrative team, needed the training as much as our teachers did. We needed to better understand just how we could provide effective feedback that encouraged teacher autonomy and empowerment. Instead of dissecting lessons with teacher groups, we asked Janie Pollock to work in tandem with principal teams to help us understand the power and value of classroom observations, common language, and effective feedback. Principals intently watched for examples of the nine high-yield instructional strategies shown by research to boost student achievement. By sharing observational experiences, we began to improve the quality of our feedback to teachers, and teachers began to seek it out. Principals approached conversations more confidently as they met with teachers to discuss how the high-yield strategies fit into the GANAG framework. We had discerned that this dialogue could make a positive difference in classroom instruction, but we recognized that this contribution was only part of the success being realized.

It has been the individual classroom teacher who has made a positive impact on learning in ways that we had not imagined. In our walkthroughs, we now routinely observe how teachers are working to find better ways to include high-yield strategies that engage students and enrich lessons. One way this is apparent is in the way teachers communicate goals. Before, we might have seen teachers post or ask students to write down the goal of the day; now we are seeing teachers provide the opportunity for students to understand the goals and to personalize them.

Here's an example shared recently by one of our observers, a middle school principal who entered a classroom while the teacher was in the midst of a lesson opener. The principal selected a student and asked him what the sentences prominently displayed on the board were. That was the lesson's goal, the student replied, and the class worked to understand a new lesson goal each day. Continuing, the principal asked if the student knew the answer to the questions within the goal. "Well, no, I don't," the student responded. "Not yet. That is what we are trying to learn."

Based on what we see, when students in our district walk into a classroom, they look for the lesson goal that's been written on the board and then begin talking about what they are about to learn. Within the first few minutes of the class period, they record the lesson's goal in their notebook and, in many cases, use an objective score sheet to document the effort they plan to put into their learning; they will revisit the goal at the end of the lesson. In this way, teachers help make the connection between effort and achievement, and the result is more students beginning to take control over their own learning. We see students who have a clear understanding of learning goals because they actively communicate with their teachers about what they are learning.

These improvements have not happened overnight, and we realize that there is plenty we need to continue to do to engage students in ways that correlate to improved student achievement. What is evident is that the initiative of the classroom teacher is allowing ongoing adjustment in instructional practice that will ultimately result in improved student achievement.

Although we are in the beginning stages of this journey, gains in achievement are evident. We will continue to work tirelessly to support and empower teachers through practices that alter pedagogical habits, because we realize that it is ultimately thoughtful change at the classroom level, rather than broad, sweeping reform at the district level, that is truly making the difference. We can now confidently work to close the student achievement gap, because we are finally properly minding that gap.

2

Solutions That Are Invisible in Plain Sight

AS EDUCATORS SEEK SOLUTIONS TO IMPROVE ACHIEVEMENT FOR students whose learning is marginalized by poverty, language, and disabilities, we can draw on both the research findings about teaching and learning and on the methods used by researchers who study the power of positive deviance. "Positive deviance" is a term used to describe the uncommon behaviors characteristic of people who beat the odds in seemingly difficult situations.

According to social behaviorist researchers Pascale, Sternin, and Sternin (2010), the unusual habits of and actions taken by so-called positive deviants enable them to find solutions to difficult problems even when their peers do not. These individuals or groups succeed in the face of challenges that others find insurmountable, and they do so using the same resources available to everyone else in their community. When researchers investigate tactics used by positive deviants and teach other members to replicate them, the positive results are immediate and long lasting (Pascale et al., 2010).

Finding solutions in schools to improve learning for academically at-risk students is a perfect scenario for using positive deviance. What if we examined the learning approaches of students who do succeed in schools and the instructional methods of teachers who work successfully with them? What techniques might we replicate? What can we learn from the effective teachers and academic achievers who succeed where their colleagues and classmates struggle?

Let's look at a couple of examples of the tenets of positive deviance before we apply it to the classroom. One critical point made by Pascale and colleagues is that very often the solutions to stubborn problems are *invisible in plain sight*, impossible to see because so much of our attention is focused elsewhere. They illustrate this idea with the following anecdote:

> The 13th-century Sufi mystic Nasrudin is a fixture in Middle Eastern folklore. His parables combine wisdom with irony, logic with the illogical, the superficial with the profound. In one tale, he is a notorious smuggler routinely crossing the frontier with his string of donkeys, saddlebags loaded with straw. Customs inspectors search in vain for the contraband that accounts for his steady accumulation of wealth. Years go by. Nasrudin retires. One day he encounters the former chief of customs in a local teahouse.
>
> The retired official broaches a long-suppressed question: "Nasrudin, as we are now old men who have ended our careers and are no longer a threat to each other, tell me, during all those years, what were you smuggling?"
>
> Nasrudin replies: "Donkeys." (Pascale et al., 2010, p. 6)

Nasrudin's tale prompts us to ask ourselves what conventional beliefs or habits may be preventing us from seeing what works in schools. The conventional way to approach school reform is to take a big-picture approach—to examine the entire school as a single system. A less conventional way to approach reform is one classroom at a time, focusing on specific tactics that individual teachers use in their own classrooms to successfully mind and close achievement gaps. The solutions are likely *invisible in plain sight*—as invisible as Nasrudin's smuggled donkeys.

Now let's consider another example of positive deviance, one that highlights how a solution identified by positive deviants became standard practice for the rest of the community.

In the 1800s, a physician named Ignaz Semmelweis hypothesized that maternal deaths by puerperal fever would be reduced from 10 percent to below 1 percent if physicians washed their hands between patients. He noticed that the midwives who attended women in childbirth washed their hands much more frequently than hospital obstetricians did. Scrutinizing the two groups, he observed that the midwives (the positive deviants) cleaned their hands repeatedly throughout the day as they took care of daily tasks such as laundry and cooking, along with birthing. The hospital physicians, by contrast, washed once in the morning and then assisted in multiple births all day without rewashing their hands. Semmelweis's resulting suggestion that physicians adopt a practice of low-status midwives, and a practice as mundane as hand washing, was ridiculed by the establishment and contributed to him losing his license to practice medicine. His vindication did not come until many years after his death, when germ theory was confirmed. Semmelweis's hand-washing guidelines are now considered the gold standard of reducing infection and continue to save lives today (Pascale et al., 2010, p. 83).

This story illustrates three key aspects of positive deviance methodology that teachers can apply to their own classroom practices.

1. *General observation*—taking an overall look at the behaviors of those people who beat the odds in the face of difficult or stubborn problems. What did the midwives, whose patients had more positive outcomes, do that the physicians, whose patients had fewer positive outcomes, did not? What solution might be invisible in plain sight?

2. *A somersault question*—turning "the norm" on its head. Here, the question might have been what, if anything, might the doctors have been doing that inadvertently contributed to maternal deaths? The physicians who were required to divide their attention between delivery and other aspects of their heavy workload could have hypothesized that a certain number deaths were to be expected.

3. *A focus on replicating specific behavior*—identifying a specific action or actions (here, frequent hand washing) and finding ways for any other member of the community, sharing the same resources and the same environment, to do the same.

As a result of observing, asking a somersault question, and identifying a replicable behavior, any member of a community can achieve the same odds-beating results as the positive deviants.

✳ Time to Reflect ✳

In what ways does the positive deviance methodology have relevance for schools today?

Positive Deviance and Classrooms

In our search for ways to increase achievement for academically at-risk students, we can draw an analogy between the stories of positive deviance and the examples we see in schools of certain students notably outperforming their peers in terms good grades and test scores, and certain teachers notably outperforming their colleagues in terms of student results on tests. (Although we may not see test scores as the most critical measure of learning success, their current status as a viable indicator of student achievement must be acknowledged.) Let's consider the three key aspects of positive deviance methodology: observation, a somersault question, and specific behaviors.

What Do Higher-Performing Students Do That Other Students Do Not?

Based on our observation, we have identified the following characteristics of positive deviant students—those who perform better than their peers:

• They know, or know how to seek out, the learning goal of every lesson, even when it is not explicitly posted or presented to the class.

• They use high-yield strategies, such as note taking, asking questions, asking for feedback from peers, and proposing new ideas or ways of carrying out tasks, even when the teacher does not direct them to do so or teach them to use those strategies.

• They seek performance feedback about their own understandings or ways of practicing skills, and seek informational feedback about how to improve or advance to a higher level.

What Might Teachers Be Doing
That Keeps Students from Performing Well?

This is an uncomfortable question but one that is absolutely necessary to ask. First, though, it is important to recognize teachers for the commendable job they do. Rising secondary school graduation rates worldwide are a tribute to the successful work of professional educators. In the United States, 76 percent of young people graduate from high school (Organisation for Economic Co-operation and Development, 2011). This figure is relevant, because positive deviance methodology works best when most of the population performs at an acceptable rate but a small percentage could improve.

The somersault question of what teachers might inadvertently be doing to hold students back has no easy answers. It is certainly true that out-of-school factors can have a very strong influence on students' in-school performance, and historically, teachers may have expected and demanded less of children whose learning is marginalized by poverty, language, and disabilities. This point of view, espoused by James Coleman and his "Coleman Report" in the 1960s, was not disputed until recently.

The research today, however, confirms teachers are the most important influence on student learning, prompting us to focus our somersault questioning on the teaching practices in each classroom. What are teachers doing, or not doing, as they go about their daily business? What could they do differently? What could they do more effectively? What new classroom techniques could they adopt to help academically at-risk students achieve more? Based on the research, we conclude that a teacher can increase student achievement by taking the following actions:

1. Making sure every student knows the learning goals and success criteria for every lesson and throughout a unit.

2. Teaching every student how to use high-yield strategies to learn content and skills and stressing the benefits of this approach, even though it can be time-consuming.

3. Ensuring every student knows how to seek and receive frequent, meaningful feedback about progress toward the curriculum targets for that grade level and subject.

Many teachers might agree with these statements and argue that they are working to do these things. When one observes classes, however, it becomes clear that only *some* students know the learning goals, only *some* students use high-yield strategies, and only *some* students know how to seek and apply feedback. Stated differently, not all teachers provide daily lesson goals with a strategy for all students to interact with the goal; not all teachers teach students to use high-yield strategies daily; and not all teachers provide opportunities for students to seek and receive feedback throughout lessons.

Focusing on Specific, Replicable Behavior

The conversation now turns to the final question: is there a technique or set of techniques (such as hand washing) that other students or teachers could replicate in order increase achievement? The answer is a definitive yes. With a few deliberate actions in preparation and delivery, any teacher can ensure that *all* students have the same opportunity and support necessary to reach proficient or advanced status on tests of standards that only some students show today. In fact, the tools a teacher needs to effect the three critical changes identified in the previous section—(1) student awareness of goals and success criteria, (2) student use of high-yield strategies in active pursuit of learning, and (3) student pursuit and use of feedback to guide that learning to a successful outcome—already exist in every classroom in the form of the curriculum document, the plan book, and the grade book.

Time to Reflect

How do you think the suggestion to change teaching habits would resonate with the teachers in your school?

A Closer Look at the Tools Teachers Have

The curriculum, the plan book, and the grade book, when strategically used in combination, empower any teacher to help any student improve, regardless of that student's baseline achievement level or out-of-school factors.

Tool #1: The Curriculum

A good basic curriculum document is a great tool: a list of standards and objectives for each grade level and each subject area that clearly and succinctly identifies what students should know and be able to do. The Common Core State Standards for English Language Arts & Literacy and for Mathematics are solid examples of strong curricula. They are the latest in an evolving series that traces back to the state standards of the late 1990s; the collections of subject-area standards from expert groups like the National Council of Teachers of Mathematics (NCTM), first seen in 1989; the outcomes of the Outcome-Based Education (OBE) era of the 1980s; and, famously, the taxonomy of educational objective edited by Benjamin Bloom in the 1950s.

The truth about curriculum documents and teachers is that the documents tend to become an anathema of school reform because of the way in which they are typically written, which is usually so complicated that they are unworkable for busy teachers. Despite the hours classroom teachers invest in writing units, most teachers can teach without referencing the official district curriculum document. Instead, teachers plan activities for students to engage in, and if they do consult standards, it is often so that they can find multiple standards that seem appropriate to the activities that have been decided on and paste them into lesson plans, usually as a concession to policy requirements.

The curriculum document should be a grade-level set of standards unpacked to objectives that lend themselves to being disseminated into units of study. For every unit, a teacher should be able to identify the underlying standards and provide them to students in a format that welcomes interactivity. The standards should be presented as clear learning targets, phrased in student-friendly language and in a way that includes specific, measurable criteria for both daily scoring and unit testing.

For example, Linda Law, a district director of curriculum and instruction, used the Common Core State Standards to convert K–12 English and math documents into a format that allows the course or grade-level teacher to view approximately 45 curriculum statements (grade-level standards, or what we will refer to later as goals). For pacing, the teachers distribute the curriculum standards among 6 to 10 units of study for the year. The standards document provides the criteria that teachers use daily in the classroom for planning lessons and for scoring student progress. In the Educator's Voice section following this chapter, Susan Hensley explains how she prepared similar documents for elementary teachers.

To recap, the invisible-in-plain-sight solution to the problem of every student *not* knowing the learning goals and *not* being aware of the success criteria for every lesson and throughout a unit is the curriculum document. The impediment is that many teachers are unaccustomed to using this document to guide their instruction. This takes us to the next tool: a teacher's plan book.

✖ Time to Reflect ✖

Examine the curriculum documents in your school for clearly stated standards and objectives. What role do these documents play in your (or your staff's) lesson planning?

Tool #2: The Plan Book

The second tool for improving instruction and learning, the plan book, provides a mechanism for teaching to the curriculum every day. In the plan book, a teacher can map out how she will deliberately teach to the goals and objectives (using highly effective instructional strategies). The way to do this is by following what Janie has dubbed the Teaching Schema for Master Learners (Pollock, 2007), a lesson planning protocol she developed by updating the approach in Madeline Hunter's *Mastery Teaching* (1982). This schema, commonly known as GANAG (an acronym for its five steps), guides teachers to plan for successful learning. The steps in a quality lesson are simple:

G Share **GOAL**/standard(s) and objective(s)
Opportunity for feedback
A **ACCESS** prior student knowledge
Opportunity for feedback
N Acquire and process **NEW INFORMATION** (procedural or declarative)
Opportunity for feedback
A **APPLY** knowledge in a new situation and create original ideas
Opportunity for feedback
G **GOAL REVIEW** or summarize
Homework and assessment

GANAG cues the teacher to start every lesson by providing the goal or curriculum standard so that students know what the lesson will enable them to understand, do, or do better. Throughout a GANAG-designed lesson, teachers provide opportunities for students to seek and receive feedback about their progress toward skill mastery or content understanding. See Figure 2.1 for a simple lesson planning template.

⚒ Time to Reflect ⚒

What lesson planning schema do teachers use in your school?

GANAG was originally conceived as a way to plan and deliver instruction that would guide all students to use high-yield strategies critical to improving academic performance. In *Classroom Instruction That Works* (Marzano et al., 2001), Janie and her colleagues presented research findings supporting the effectiveness of nine instructional strategies—those found to exceed 0.5 standard deviations and thus shown to have a significant impact on learning outcomes. This group of strategies, familiar to many teachers, comprises the following:

1. Identify similarities and differences ($d = 1.61$)
2. Summarize and take notes ($d = 1.00$)
3. Recognize effort and provide recognition ($d = 0.80$)

FIGURE 2.1
The GANAG Lesson Planning Template

Lesson Title:

G	
A	
N	**Acquire and Process New Information**
	Declarative　　　　　　　　　　　Procedural
A	**Use Higher-Order Processing Skills**
	Thinking Skills　　　　　　Practice – Shape – New Situation
G	

4. Provide homework and practice ($d = 0.75$)

5. Use nonlinguistic representations ($d = 0.75$)

6. Use cooperative learning ($d = 0.73$)

7. Set objectives and provide feedback ($d = 0.61$)

8. Generate and test hypotheses ($d = 0.61$)

9. Use questions, cues, and advance organizers ($d = 0.59$)

Although many teachers may recognize the list of effective strategies, many also think of them solely as *teaching* techniques—ways to present content to students. What these teachers might not have considered, though, is that these strategies are also *learning* strategies to be employed by both teachers *and* students. Teachers can show students how to carry out these strategies themselves and can structure lessons so that students employ these strategies in class every day.

Earlier we asked the somersault question of whether or not teachers could inadvertently be contributing to low achievement. Ginny McElhaney, a principal in a K–12 school in Tennessee, asked that question, too. Through observation, Ginny saw that many students in her school were quite adept at using the nine high-yield strategies, which teachers had been trained to incorporate into instruction and classroom activities. And she discovered that the students who *were not* adept at these strategies were the ones who were chronically underachieving and unmotivated. Ginny investigated and learned that although teachers said they were using high-yield strategies, they were not deliberately teaching their students to do so.

Could it be, Ginny wondered, that what unmotivated, underachieving, and low-performing students needed was nothing more than *explicit instruction* on how to summarize, how to use nonlinguistic representations, how to generate and test hypotheses, and so on? She and her staff immediately committed to finding ways to teach *every* student to use the strategies every day in class. The solution they were looking for had been available to them the whole time, but for some reason, they just had not seen it. "It was like finding Waldo," Ginny remembers. "Once you saw him, in his striped red-and-white shirt, you wondered how you had not seen him all along."

The five-stage GANAG lesson planning and delivery schema cues teac[h]ers to plan lessons that deliberately teach and provide time for students to use the strategies daily, at certain stages in the lesson. For example:

G **GOAL**/standard or objective stage
Set objectives and provide feedback.
Recognize effort and provide recognition.

A **ACCESS PRIOR KNOWLEDGE** stage
Identify similarities and differences.
Use nonlinguistic representations.
Use cooperative learning.
Use questions, cues, and advance organizers.

N **NEW INFORMATION** stage
Summarize and take notes.
Provide practice.
Use cooperative learning.
Use questions, cues, and advance organizers.

A **APPLY** stage
Identify similarities and differences.
Provide practice.
Generate and test hypotheses.
Use questions, cues, and advance organizers.

G **GOAL REVIEW** or summarize stage
Set objectives and provide feedback.
Recognize effort and provide recognition.

As students use the high-yield strategies daily to engage with the lesson content, they have continual opportunities to seek and receive feedback about the progress they are making toward lesson goals—the standards and daily objectives. Of course, in addition to planning for instruction and formative assessment, the teacher gives tests or assigns other forms of assessment, such as projects, in order to make a summative judgment about student performance.

⚔ Time to Reflect ⚔

How might reconceptualizing the familiar high-yield strategies as learning strategies rather than solely teaching techniques change your instructional approaches?

Gretchen Lee, who teaches 3rd grade, had this to say about revisiting daily lesson planning through the lens of GANAG:

> I've been shocked by how foreign it seems to sit down to plan any kind of daily structure and really prepare for what will happen in my class. I consider myself a very reflective practitioner, but I guess I had bought into the myth that as you get more experience, lesson planning is not really needed. At least, you certainly don't have to write down your delivery. I believed that I was doing a lot of the steps that are explicitly laid out in GANAG: remembering to set the goals, planning a hook, and so on. But what I've come to realize is that I most likely wasn't.
>
> Well, now GANAG prompts me to create a much more structured daily lesson and reminds me that my students need deliberate feedback related to the lesson objective. I've learned that feedback techniques that were automatic to me are not as meaningful for my students as I thought they were. Even worse, some students were using the strategies when the others didn't, and I'm embarrassed to admit that I did not think it was my responsibility as much as their parents' responsibility that these students weren't making progress.
>
> I'd forgotten how difficult it is to change old habits. Changing my instruction planning and delivery has caused me to confront two major issues: (1) my lesson planning for the past four or five years has been more of "lesson outlining," and (2) my record keeping has not been providing me with useful data, because I was not deliberately providing opportunities for feedback to the lesson goals and then tracking the data showing student improvement toward these goals.

It honestly did not occur to me that I could change student learning significantly on a daily basis, thus making long-term changes that would
impact state test data. But I could. And I have. Now my students are performing better, and I'm hooked.

There are many dedicated teachers like Gretchen in schools—teachers
who are willing to use the simple solutions such as a planning schema to
adjust their practice and significantly mind the achievement gap in their
own classrooms.

❊ Time to Reflect ❊

Does Gretchen's reflection sound familiar to you or would it seem familiar to
your colleagues?

Tool #3: The Grade Book

The third powerful and too-often-overlooked tool teachers have at their
disposal is the grade book, the place to document both ongoing or formative
assessment (such as assignments and informal observation) and summative
assessment tasks (such as tests or projects).

Vanessa Trujillo-Smith, a student teacher, once called Janie to ask for
advice. "I feel really prepared to teach," Vanessa said, "but I honestly do not feel
the same way about assessment and grading. Please help me understand why
I'm struggling with this, and then how to do assessment and grading right."

Teaching is, in some regard, a cultural activity that begins with playing
school and going to school, and critical aspects of teaching that are culturally
learned are often taken for granted (Stigler & Hiebert, 1998). We begin learning
how to teach by watching our own teachers, from kindergarten through college. One thing we could not learn by watching teachers was how to assess and
grade students—because this is something that went on behind the scenes. It
is also worth remembering that the original purpose of assessment was sorting
students, and the original purpose of grading was to promote better schools.

We recommend that educators interested in assessment read the riveting history of assessment and grading presented in Guskey and Bailey's *Developing Grading and Reporting Systems for Student Learning* (2000) and the iconic *Wad-Ja-Get? The Grading Game in American Education,* by Kirschenbaum, Napier, and Simon (1971).

When Vanessa asked for help, we first focused on how she could use the curriculum standards (the "Gs" in her daily lessons) to track student progress during instruction. Using a simple spreadsheet, with the student roster down the side and the standards across the top, she could organize activity grades by student and by standard. Now, during instruction, Vanessa walks around with a goal sheet on her clipboard (the way that her softball coach used to do on the field, charting players' skill proficiency as they learned and practiced skills), interacting with students, observing their work, and making marks on her standard- and student-focused goal sheet. This live scoring process, called "standards-based scoring" or "standards-based grading," generates real-time feedback for Vanessa and the students about progress toward goals. It also captures patterns in the individual and class data to inform decisions about pacing, differentiation, and planning for subsequent lessons. Vanessa then transfers the informally collected data into her grade book, which is organized by standards rather than by an assignment-by-assignment chronology.

Although grading and record-keeping procedures are a bit more detailed than this anecdote conveys, we like the way Vanessa's story stresses the elegant simplicity of gathering data related to student progress toward standards (the "Gs" of GANAG) and being able to share those data with students to provide feedback. Viewing all assignments and observations as opportunities for formative assessment can reveal patterns predictive of student performances on tests and other summative tasks. For a teacher who is following the structure of GANAG, this way of using the grade book completes a sequence that started with connecting the curriculum to the plan book, and connecting the plan book to the recording and grading of student progress. These three tools, used in this manner, help teachers to be more mindful and to more effectively enable student learning.

⋈ Time to Reflect ⋈

How could you change your grading to include standards-based scoring?

Updating the Educational Framework

Teachers are familiar with the long-established educational framework of Curriculum-Instruction-Assessment (C-I-A). The somersault question we have asked is, "Is there something about teaching to C-I-A that inadvertently contributes to low achievement for some students?"

We believe the answer to this question is yes. The traditional C-I-A framework prompts teachers to identify the content they teach, plan and deliver their instruction, and test periodically. Invisible in plain sight is that C-I-A emphasizes *the teacher and the teaching* rather than *the students and the learning*. For this reason, we believe the traditional and unquestionably valuable "C-I-A approach" can be updated to clarify the direct impact the curriculum, instruction, and assessment have on all learners' progress, and this means expanding to include the critical fourth component of *goal-related feedback*. This is the purpose of the Big Four framework, which emerged from Janie's work in updating the C-I-A framework. It calls for teachers to do the following:

1. *Use well-articulated curriculum standards,* with modified learning targets (IEPs and English Language Frameworks) for special populations.

2. *Plan for delivery,* asking every student to use high-yield instructional strategies.

3. *Vary assessment* to help learners "form" learning (employ formative assessment and view progress toward the curriculum standards) in addition to providing summative assessment tasks.

4. *Document feedback as standards-based scores* on charts and in grade books to capture trends as well as averages; teach students to monitor their own progress, as well.

As Janie has noted in one of her previous books,

Many teachers are likely to say that they are already implementing [the individual elements of] the Big Four. Certainly they have a curriculum, create lesson plans, use some different assessment techniques, and give feedback in the form of grades. But if we ask these same teachers if all their students perform to their expectations, we might get a very different set of reactions—possibly including some that shift the blame for failure to the students: "I did my best, but the students didn't do their part." (Pollock, 2007, p. 8)

The Big Four calls on teachers to intentionally use curriculum standards to guide, instruct, assess, and communicate student progress in a way that will help every student learn better, even those whose learning is marginalized by poverty, language barriers, and disabilities. Research shows that deliberately teaching and assessing to the curriculum objectives results in student gains that exceed performance commensurate with gains generally found among students of higher socioeconomic status. It also confirms that learning improves when students are made aware of curriculum goals and receive personal and frequent feedback related to their progress toward those goals (Marzano et al., 2001). When the teacher writes standards and objectives from the curriculum on the board, she should intend to have students interact with those goals, plan for students to engage in activities that increase their knowledge and skills about those goals, and ensure that students receive frequent feedback during instruction and through testing so they can gauge their progress toward those goals.

❈ Time to Reflect ❈

How do you see the addition of goal-related feedback affecting the use of C-I-A?

A New Look at Feedback

Ten years ago, social studies teacher Gary Nunnally admitted that he was frustrated by the fact that his students did not work as hard as he did. For years, he planned and delivered lessons, but there were about five students in every class who passively went through the motions. Gary spent an inordinate amount of time addressing these students' lack of interest. He wrote to and met with their parents, he took points off their assignments, and he warned them that they were jeopardizing their academic future.

But then Gary found a solution for teaching academically at-risk students by examining the learning behaviors of his successful students. Those students, he noticed, asked questions, negotiated grades, and asked friends for help to understand material both in class and outside class. In short, they knew how to "do school" very well. Gary saw his challenge as getting all of his students to adopt these positive deviant behaviors. If you ask him now what one change was most instrumental in that effort and has had the biggest positive effect on his classroom teaching, he will say, "It was feedback."

This might not seem like a particularly "positive deviant" response; after all, both the benefits of feedback and ways of providing it are well established. As Gary points out, it would be difficult to find a teacher who does not give feedback to students; it's a basic feature of the job. Teachers give daily assignment grades and marks on tests. They provide written comments on papers and projects. Teachers provide verbal comments during discussions as they call on students to answer questions. Gary notes that any teachers told to generate more feedback for students are likely to reply that they don't need to—and that they wouldn't have time to, anyway, as they are already taxed for time trying to cover required content. Telling teachers to use feedback in their classrooms feels a bit like telling modern doctors to wash their hands; they would say, "Of course! We already do!"

Again we might ask a somersault question and look at "normal" feedback practices in a new way. What if teachers did not have to be the only source for feedback? What if feedback, with all its research-proven benefits, could come from somewhere else? What if *students* could learn to actively seek feedback, or at least receive and benefit from feedback from someone other than the teacher?

Students Seeking Feedback

Students who perform well in school seek and manage feedback for themselves; they don't always wait for someone else to give it to them. These are the behaviors of positive deviants, and the question is whether or not all students can learn to seek feedback. We believe they can.

Setting objectives and providing feedback is one of the high-yield strategies explained in the meta-analysis that Janie and her colleagues published in the book *Classroom Instruction That Works* (Marzano et al., 2001). John Hattie's (2009) meta-analyses also identified feedback as the single most important factor to impact student learning.

It is helpful to think about instructional feedback from the student's perspective rather than from the teacher's and as something *sought* rather than as something *given*. From this point of view, there are various sources of feedback available in a classroom:

• Traditional *expert feedback* from the teacher, such as instructional comments or cues to steer or direct thinking in a certain direction, comments on written assignments, and corrections on tests.

• *Clarifying feedback* from peers, such as the kind of discussions that emerge from pair-sharing arrangements or viewing others' notes or products in order to see another form of a product.

• *Reflective feedback* that students generate themselves, such as metacognitive deliberations, or thoughts that are triggered by prompts embedded in material (e.g., computer-assisted instruction, and online text, images, and interactions), and journals or note taking.

• *Listening-in feedback* from others, including what students see or overhear about lesson content or other student performances.

In an instructional setting, feedback can be any information related to a curriculum standard that motivates a student to improve his knowledge or skill. Embracing this definition opens a teacher's eyes to feedback as something students can learn to use in class to check both their understanding and their progress relative to curriculum standards and objectives. The teacher's role shifts from generating all of the feedback during and after lessons to providing opportunities and explicit direction for students to seek feedback throughout a lesson, reflect on it, and apply it formatively to self-monitor, engage in additional practice, and seek and receive more goal-related information.

Providing Opportunities for Feedback

Teaching students to actively seek and use feedback involves the following:

- Modeling how to self-assess and self-correct in light of feedback.
- Maximizing opportunities to provide students with clarification to aid their interpretation of feedback or teaching them to ask follow-up questions to get that clarification for themselves.
- Managing class time and resources to allow students sufficient opportunity to seek and use feedback in class.

Any student can learn to initiate the process of seeking feedback in a classroom where the teacher explicitly provides opportunities and direction to do so. However, this approach to using feedback is dependent on the teachers' approach to other teaching and learning practices. The most critical of these is setting the goal. As our colleague Trent Scott says, "There is no such thing as good feedback to a bad set of goals" (in Pollock, 2012, p. 87).

⚒ Time to Reflect ⚒

How might changing the ways students seek and receive feedback alter your current teaching practices?

Seeing Solutions in the Data

"We recognized our need to make achievement gains in rural schools here in the Tri-County North region in Ohio," says Joanele Hoce, a district director of curriculum and intervention support. "Our focus on school improvement, driven by No Child Left Behind federal legislation, was all about testing and low results, with too little emphasis on recognizing indicators of progress the low-achieving students were making along the way or the strategies that were in place for students showing desired achievement gains. This left us with a lot of data but few solutions about how to close the achievement gaps we identified." This bolstered the conventional belief that there was little an individual teacher could do to overcome the socioeconomic and demographic factors affecting each child.

Joanele realized that her county schools had data, but not a framework for improvement. She and her team used research to change teaching and to view data differently. Teachers needed fresh ideas. Teachers needed to know how to *do something* about the low scores their school continued to generate, rather than just acknowledge them and continue to gather similar data next year. Teachers needed the "how," and the conventional data provided more of the "what." As it turned out, the teachers needed to use the tools of curriculum, instruction, and assessment that had been in front of them all along, *invisible in plain sight,* and they needed to learn to use these tools differently.

"As we analyze data now," Joanele says, "we are able to identify the causal factors that have resulted in the positive gains and effects that lead straight back to the teachers who changed their habits and embraced the Big Four, GANAG, high-yield strategies, and a different approach to grading by standards. Using software to show growth within the school year, called value-added data, we showed the quality of the teacher in the classroom who transformed his or her pedagogy through purposeful planning, intentional teaching with goal-related feedback, and helping students to become master learners who use the high-yield strategies every day."

After a year of changing teaching habits and using a newer progress measure that isolated incremental and continuous growth within the mass of student test information collected, Joanele and her team were able to see the gains. "Prior to working with value-added data, we had many opinions but little evidence that we were meeting the needs of all students."

✥ Time to Reflect ✥

How does positive deviance methodology and Joanele Hoce's discussion of assessment data relate to your school's efforts to improve student achievement?

Moving Forward with a Few New Teaching and Learning Practices

One important characteristic of the research method of positive deviance is that social complexity or cultural habits often inhibit members of a community from seeing ways to make positive changes and even solve problems that plague their group. Without question, teachers have successfully used curriculum documents, plan books, and grade books for many generations, and most students have benefitted from these practices. What was *invisible in plain sight* was that adding goal-related feedback as the pivotal change to the C-I-A framework encourages every teacher to plan and give opportunities for goal-related feedback in every lesson.

Each of the next chapters focuses on practical methods for using goal-based feedback with academically at-risk students and *all* students in a classroom. All of the recommendations involve teachers intentionally doing the following:

- Providing learning goals and asking academically at-risk students to interact with these goals.
- Purposefully planning for students to use high-yield learning strategies.
- Maximizing feedback to engage students throughout instruction.

To provide the learning goals and a strategy for students to interact with the goal, we suggest that teachers teach students to use an objective score sheet (OSS). This self-assessment tool is introduced in Chapter 3 as part of teaching students to use interactive notebooks. In Chapter 4, the objective score sheet is adapted for English language learners using the English language learning standards in the state frameworks. In Chapter 5, special education students use modified goal sheets that are consistent with their individualized education plans (IEPs) and carefully monitored by specialists; however, the content goals for these students are the same as the content goals for all other students.

In each of these chapters, we recommend ways to teach students to use high-yield strategies, guided by the GANAG or GANAGPlus protocol, in the planning and delivery of lessons. Each chapter describes ways that teachers can maximize feedback by involving students in self-assessment and in tracking their own progress toward the curriculum goals. We also share ways for teachers to assess and document that student progress using tools as simple as a clipboard and a class roster.

Educator Voice

Susan Hensley, Elementary Curriculum Specialist

For Susan Hensley, helping teachers and instructional coaches use the curriculum made it very evident that the various subject-area groups had great ways to make gains, but they seemed not to blend or even "talk the same language." The turning point for her came when she started using the Big Four and showing her colleagues how, when supported with the nine high-yield strategies, it could help them organize and focus their daily work in a way that improved student learning. Incorporation of the Big Four and researched learning strategies provided a foundation for what Susan and the educators working with her found to be the cornerstone of student progress—students actively seeking feedback and incorporating it daily in their work toward learning goals.

Creating Master Learners

Like so many of my friends and colleagues, I have been working for most of my teaching career to close the elusive achievement gap. In fact, "closing the gap" has been the subject of almost every back-to-school meeting and new initiative that has come down the pike. Whether working as a classroom teacher, literacy facilitator, or curriculum specialist, I have clung tightly to the pendulum as it has swung through national reform movements such as whole language, direct instruction, balanced literacy, and now the Common Core State Standards (CCSS). Millions of dollars have been spent on districtwide and schoolwide interventions designed to help underachieving learners catch up with their peers. With so much time, energy, and money being spent, I can't help but wonder, "Why is the gap not yet closed?"

In May 2010, in a new effort to increase student achievement, my school district began providing professional development sessions on the Big Four—an approach aimed at improving learning outcomes through focused teacher attention on curriculum, instructional planning and delivery, varied assessment practices, and the use of criterion-based feedback. To my surprise, these sessions were about much more than increasing test scores; they introduced a way of teaching designed to help all children learn better every day, regardless of the challenges they faced.

In our first meeting, Janie Pollock introduced the idea of shifting our focus from being "master teachers" to creating "master learners." Such a simple idea, but such a *powerful* one. My goal has always been to help teachers become more effective; however, I have long assumed that as the knowledge and skill level of the teachers I work with increases, student achievement will increase as well. In my role as a curriculum specialist, I have come to understand how focusing on student work when working with teachers reenergizes our conversations, but also is a safe back door into great discussions about what is happening in classrooms.

Seeing with New Eyes

There is a fading half-sheet of paper stuck to the file cabinet in my office. It has the following quote typed on it:

> The voyage of discovery is not in seeking new landscapes but in having new eyes.
>
> — *Marcel Proust*

I came across this quote at a time when I was struggling to schedule an impossible number of teachers into a limited number of professional development sessions. I had to change the schedule completely four different times before it worked, and each version forced me to look at the schedule differently—through "new eyes." As our work with Janie continued, I realized that she was asking us to do the very same thing. If we were going to close the gap in our district, we were going to have to take Proust's advice and look at our teaching with "new eyes."

When I think about improving student achievement, I immediately see teachers and think about schoolwide or districtwide professional development. My goal of improving student achievement does not need to change. But what must change is my gaze: my perception of and focus on the learners and what is happening in the classroom.

"Organizing My Closet"

My state adopted and has begun implementing the Common Core State Standards (CCSS). As our district moves forward with the process of revising report cards and curriculum documents, we face the challenges of helping teachers understand what this move to the CCSS means. If we aren't careful, the new standards could be perceived as just "yet another new initiative" competing for their attention. But our ace in the hole is the Big Four, which is providing the structure for our new big picture.

I am very fortunate to work in a district that provides quality professional development opportunities for its teachers, but every rose has its thorn. Each year, there are a number of professional development programs offered to our elementary teachers. Even though the overarching goal for our district's professional development is improving student achievement, the number of new teaching strategies we are advocating can be confusing and overwhelming.

I remember that as a classroom teacher, when I learned a new teaching strategy, I threw it in my "strategy closet," and before I was introduced to the Big Four, my closet was a mess. Strategies, documents, and techniques were thrown into one big pile that I had to dig through, trying to find the one most appropriate for a situation. The process was not very efficient, and I didn't always choose the best strategy to meet the differentiated needs of students.

Today, as I work with teachers, I realize that the Big Four framework has provided organizing "shelves" for my closet (numbered 1–4, below) and for theirs, too. These shelves help teachers more effectively use their teaching tools of curriculum goals, plan books, and grade books. Now, instead of a jumbled pile of documents, strategies, and initiatives, their closets are organized something like this:

1. Using a well-articulated curriculum
   a. State standards/Common Core Standards
   b. Our previous curriculum documents and maps
   c. Common Core curriculum maps
   d. Unit planners
2. Planning for lesson delivery
   a. Plan book using GANAG
   b. High-yield strategies
   c. Sheltered Instruction Observation Protocol (SIOP) strategies
   d. Co-teaching
   e. Cooperative learning
   f. Cognitive Guided Instruction (CGI)
   g. Interactive electronic whiteboard techniques
3. Varying assessment strategies
   a. Assessment notebook
   b. Developmental Spelling Assessment
   c. STAR Reading/STAR Math
   d. The Learning Institute (TLI) quarterly assessments
   e. Criterion-referenced test/norm-referenced test (CRT/NRT)
4. Providing criterion-based feedback
   a. Report cards/progress reports
   b. Assessment wall
   c. Traditional testing reports (STAR, CRT/NRT, TLI)
   d. Student self-scoring rubrics
   e. Conferring techniques
   f. Clipboard checklists
   g. Grade book for record keeping

Feedback, Feedback, Feedback

Using the Big Four has helped me shift my focus back to what is happening in the classroom with individual students. Now, when teachers and I open the closet, all the components work together and have a purpose. Before, I may have reached in my closet and pulled out a strategy to share with a teacher for use in delivering a lesson without giving much thought to the rest of the picture—curriculum, assessment, and especially feedback. Now I understand that to increase student achievement, I need to consider *every* shelf for *every* lesson.

This is an exciting time to be an educator. The adoption of the CCSS is a call for significant change in our teaching practices. We are looking at our curriculum practices through "new eyes," focusing primarily on what students should be performing rather than only on what teachers should be teaching. Feedback is playing a significant role in this shift. Using the Big Four as an organizational structure, we have begun work on new curriculum documents with clear learning goals that support feedback between teachers and students.

Our previous curriculum documents were riddled with "ongoing" standards. The number of standards teachers were held responsible for in each grading period far exceeded the recommended number, which was approximately 45. We are now using the Common Core Curriculum Mapping Project Units (www.commoncore.org) to create documents that pace the new standards according to their appearance in the six-week units. Each of the units has a sophisticated theme and an essential question that frames opportunities for the depth of engagement called for in the Common Core. This new approach focuses on measuring and providing feedback based on a specific set of standards unique to each unit. Now teachers can print a one- to two-page document that lists the standards they will be using for planning lesson goals and scoring student progress within each unit. The pacing guides (see the example on p. 52) ensure that each standard will be scored at least once at some point during the school year.

In an effort to support criterion-based feedback, we have created scoring guides to accompany our pacing guides for each unit. We modeled our scoring guides after Figure 5.1 (p. 108) in *Improving Student Learning One Student*

Second Grade Unit 3	**Common Core Unit Pacing Guide**
	Building Bridges with Unlikely Friends In this six-week unit, students explore both literal and figurative bridges.

Reading Standards for Literature

RL.2.3 Describe how characters in a story respond to major events and challenges.

RL.2.4 Describe how words and phrases (e.g., regular beats, alliteration, rhymes, repeated lines) supply rhythm and meaning in a story, poem, or song.

RL.2.7 Use information gained from the illustrations and words in a print or digital text to demonstrate understanding of its characters, setting, or plot.

Reading Standards for Informational Text

RI.2.3 Describe the connection between a series of historical events, scientific ideas or concepts, or steps in technical procedures in a text.

RI.2.6 Identify the main purpose of a text, including what the author wants to answer, explain, or describe.

Writing Standards

W.2.2 Write informative/explanatory texts in which they introduce a topic, use facts and definitions to develop points, and provide a concluding statement or section.

W.2.5 With guidance and support from adults and peers, focus on a topic and strengthen writing as needed by revising and editing.

W.2.6 With guidance and support from adults, use a variety of digital tools to produce and publish writing, including in collaboration with peers.

Speaking and Listening Standards

SL.2.1 Participate in collaborative conversations with diverse partners about grade 2 topics and texts with peers and adults in small and larger groups.

   c. Ask for clarification and further explanation as needed about the topics and texts under discussion.

SL.2.6 Produce complete sentences when appropriate to task and situation in order to provide requested detail or clarification.

Language Standards

L.2.1 Demonstrate command of the conventions of standard English grammar and usage when writing or speaking.

   a. Use collective nouns (e.g., group).

L.2.2 Demonstrate command of the conventions of standard English capitalization, punctuation, and spelling when writing.

   b. Use commas in greetings and closings of letters.

   d. Generalize learned spelling patterns when writing words (e.g., cage → badge; boy → boil).

L.2.4 Determine or clarify the meaning of unknown and multiple-meaning words and phrases based on grade 2 reading and content, choosing flexibly from an array of strategies.

   d. Use knowledge of the meaning of individual words to predict the meaning of compound words (e.g., birdhouse, lighthouse, housefly; bookshelf, notebook, bookmark).

   e. Use glossaries and beginning dictionaries, both print and digital, to determine or clarify the meaning of words and phrases.

Courtesy of Rogers Public Schools, Rogers, Arkansas

at a Time (Pollock, 2007). Because the elementary schools in our district use a standards-based report card system, we added a row on our scoring guide to illustrate the connection between our report card descriptors and the standards being measured.

Learning about the Big Four while beginning the implementation process of the Common Core State Standards has been fortuitous. Both emphasize the shift from master teachers to master learners. The standards are requiring the shift, and the Big Four is helping us to make an authentic change. I feel like I have truly begun the voyage of discovery to improving student learning. Using the Big Four and ensuring that students seek and receive effective feedback within this context, our voyage is definitely not about seeking new landscapes; it is about using a new set of eyes.

3

Students at Risk:
Increasing Engagement
Through Intentional Teaching

"THERE IS NO SINGLE REASON WHY STUDENTS DROP OUT OF HIGH school," write the authors of *The Silent Epidemic: Perspectives of High School Dropouts* (Civic Enterprises & Peter Hart Research Associates, 2006), a study of young people in 25 different locations in the United States. Among the various reasons the subjects surveyed cited for dropping out were "a lack of connection to the school environment; a perception that school is boring; feeling unmotivated; academic challenges; and the weight of real world events" (p. 4).

Jenn Sykora teaches high school in St. Louis, Missouri, and many of her students come from low-income households. She addressed their lack of connection to the classroom and low motivation by using research to convince herself to change her teaching. For many years, Jenn says, she accepted the notion that one reality of high school was that some students would participate and some students would not. Some students would be motivated to work hard, and others would simply not be interested. Some would take notes, and others would refuse to do so. Jenn explains that she used to believe that the way to motivate nonparticipating students was by taking away points and lowering their grades. Today she admits that this kind of approach probably hurt her academically at-risk students more than it ever helped them. It certainly did not increase their participation, effort, or achievement.

Jenn's turning point was recognizing the positive deviants in her classes: the students who were organized. They engaged readily and enthusiastically in academic conversations, in part because they were able to go back over notes and other previous class resources they had kept in folders or notebooks. Somewhere along the line, these students had learned to do school well.

The first step for teachers who learn how to mind the gap in their own classrooms is to realize that if they are going to get all of their students to meet the curriculum goals, they must find a way to teach all of their students effectively—even the students who do not seem to want to be taught. The second critical step is to find a way to help all students connect with and participate in lessons, even when they do not think they want to connect and participate. A useful solution is teaching students to keep an interactive notebook. When used in connection with effectively structured lessons, this simple, invisible-in-plain-sight classroom resource can be a game changer for all students, especially underachieving ones.

IN9: The High-Yield Interactive Notebook

Search the Internet for "interactive notebook," and you will see examples for most subject areas. "INs" were introduced approximately 40 years ago by a textbook company and popularized by the *History Alive* curriculum. Although an "interactive notebook" may sound like a technological widget, and although it can indeed be electronic in 1:1 laptop schools where students have access to the technology, it is most often as low-tech as a spiral notebook. Folders can serve the same purpose for younger students, and three-ring binders work well for some high school courses. Despite the interactive notebook's "throwback" simplicity, it is a powerful tool that changes learning habits.

The IN9 is set up in a specific format to maximize students' involvement in their learning. The term "interactive" in the name refers to students interacting with the content and other resources, communicating with teachers and peers; think of "interactive" here as synonymous with "engagement." Going forward, we will refer to the notebooks as "IN9s" to highlight how regularly and deliberately using research-substantiated, high-yield strategies that position students to seek and receive feedback boosts the efficacy of the interactive-notebook approach. Although the research on the nine high-yield strategies was conducted prior to 2001, it still holds up well in practice; however, we have updated the discussion here to incorporate more recently published research on the power of teacher clarity and teacher-student relationships.

Interactivity to Promote Teacher Clarity and Positive Teacher-Student Relationships

Ask Jenn Sykora why she "GANAGs" her lessons, and she will tell you that the clear structure GANAG gives her instruction has helped her become a more effective teacher. This outcome is substantiated by research. Hattie (2009) cites a 1990 meta-analysis by Frank Fendick that associates teachers' organization (which includes giving clear explanations and examples during teaching and assessment) with a very strong effect on student outcomes ($d = 0.75$). Hattie editorializes that "teachers using particular teaching methods, with high expectations for all students" are likely to see above-average gains in achievement (p. 126). Using GANAG calls both teachers' and students' attention to high expectations for each step of learning. It ensures they know the goal to be achieved, the means by which to seek feedback related to the goal, the ways to track progress, and the expected assessment methods that will measure achievement.

Jenn's experience attests to that point. Now, she deliberately structures lessons to ensure that she always does the following:

G: Sets and presents a learning **GOAL** in a manner that students can understand.

A: Conducts an activity to help students **ACCESS** their prior knowledge.

N: Presents and helps students acquire the **NEW INFORMATION** related to the lesson goal.

A: Gives students the opportunity to **APPLY** a thinking skill or practice using their new knowledge in a new situation.

G: Concludes the lesson by prompting students to engage in **GOAL REVIEW,** generalizing their understandings and reviewing their progress toward the goal.

In each stage of a lesson, Jenn is careful to cue and teach students to use high-yield instructional strategies; she also plans each lesson stage to include opportunities for the students to learn new concepts and skills while seeking and receiving feedback—from her, from peers, or through self-reflection. You can read more about Jenn's approach, in her own words, in the Educator Voice beginning on page 82.

The interactive notebook is the student-directed companion to GANAG; much of its power comes from the fact that it is "student owned and operated." Teachers like Jenn dedicate class time to teaching students how to organize the material so they can use it during various lessons and refer to it throughout the school year. Students design the notebook as their own "learning space"—a place where they record daily lesson objectives, take notes as they gather information about learning goals, file completed assignments, and find the material they need to study for formal and informal assessments. In this way, interactive notebooks promote independent learning while also enabling students to share with others. The contents of the notebook support reflection on and productive communication about the student's progress. Like a baseball box score that allows a knowledgeable fan to re-create the events of a ballgame, an interactive notebook allows a student, a parent, and a teacher to re-create achievement progress related to specific lesson objectives. For all of these reasons, interactive notebooks are invaluable for students who need an instructional boost, but they should be part of every student's repertoire.

As Jenn Sykora puts it, "This kind of notebook is not for recording information so that students can cram for a test the night before. It's a way for them to learn consistently and systematically every day. My students know that their notebooks are their own work under construction. They make corrections, generate questions, and record all of it in their own words and their own handwriting in their notebooks." When an IN9 dovetails with a teacher's lesson in the GANAG format, it becomes a powerful way to increase achievement. As students adopt foundational, positive learning habits, such as note taking and taking time to organize their own work, engagement in class becomes more natural to them.

When students learn to use the notebooks interactively, the work they exhibit gives teachers insight into both successes and struggles. This ongoing window into what individual students understand about a lesson, expressed in each student's own words, allows teachers to see where their instruction is working and where it is falling short. This can lead to more effective reteaching, better differentiation, and more valuable enrichment.

On a more fundamental level, the use of interactive notebooks simply helps teachers know their students better as people and as learners. Hattie (2009) identified teacher-student relationships as having a very high effect on student achievement ($d = 0.72$), pointing out, "Building relations with students implies agency, efficacy, [and] respect by the teacher for what the child brings to the class (from home, culture, peers)" (p. 118). It is easy to see how this feeling of being respected and valued can increase a student's confidence, investment in the classroom, and motivation to succeed. In short, interactive notebooks can help teachers teach as much as they help reluctant learners learn—which, Jenn Sykora reports, was something she and her colleagues had not expected.

✄ Time to Reflect ✄

What advantages and challenges do you see to using interactive notebooks as the student companion to lessons organized around GANAG?

The rest of this chapter is divided into two parts. First, we will explain a few practical tips about setting up a notebook to increase students' organizational skills and efficiency. Then, in the second part of the chapter, we will examine how the student experiences a lesson that follows the GANAG schema and how the lesson stages are actively reflected in the student's interactive notebook.

Preparing and Personalizing an Interactive Notebook

Giving students guidance about how to set up a notebook levels the playing field for all. Significantly, it provides those who are at risk of academic failure with the kind of structure that can help them interact more effectively *with* new content and with others *about* the content. Teachers who use IN9s know it is essential to give students time and clear directions for how to prepare the notebooks and how to set up special pages for specific purposes.

Middle school teacher Tammy Lang and her colleagues created notebook guidelines to help students organize their class materials. At Tammy's school, all teachers in all subjects teach students to keep interactive notebooks, and the guidelines provide a degree of uniformity that contributes to efficiency. "Referring to guidelines is a tangible way to give students positive feedback about organizational habits; it also helps students take pride in their work," Tammy told us. "I now give students more precise feedback keyed to the guidelines rather than just general praise. And students get ideas from other student notebooks since they are organized in a similar way."

The notebooks (or folders, or binders) usually include the following:

• Personalized covers—for both the notebook as a whole and individual unit dividers
   • A page numbering system
   • A table of contents
   • A way to arrange specialized pages: vocabulary pages, quizzes, and objective score sheets

Let's take a closer look some at these common components of IN9s and the value they can bring.

Personalized Covers and Unit Dividers

Elementary school teacher Rebecca Day notes, "Personalizing or creating a notebook cover may seem like busywork, but it's a way to teach students to begin to 'own' their work. It is a statement that 'taking notes' is for them, not for you. Many of my students do not have help with schoolwork outside of school, so this elevates the importance of their work."

Jennie Hensgen, a science teacher, allowed her students to use half of a class period to design notebook covers and unit dividers, and she originally felt somewhat guilty about this decision, given the expansive science curriculum she knew she had to cover. But, Jennie admits, "Once my 7th graders had personalized their covers, they didn't want to lose their notebooks! Students would come in early to glue or staple in the assignments, but they didn't want to risk losing or ruining their books."

Asking students to design individualized unit dividers within the notebooks can further students' sense of ownership, but it has instructional benefits as well. Over the course of the unit, students can add visual summaries of the content to the divider design.

✖ Time to Reflect ✖

How do you think your underachieving students would benefit from explicit instruction about how to organize an interactive notebook and use it regularly?

A Page Numbering System

Having a uniform numbering system is advisable, as it helps all students more easily locate information from previous lessons, supporting efficiency in pair-share activities or other collaborative learning situations.

There are many ways to number the pages of an interactive notebook. For example, students might use a numerical sequence for the right-side pages (1, 2, 3, etc.) and use a corresponding alphabetical sequence for pages on the left (1A, 1B, 2A, 2B, or simply A, B, C, etc.). The numerical sequence can start over at the beginning of each unit or can be continuous throughout the notebook. If the numbering sequence repeats for each unit, it may be helpful to identify a specific sequence by prefacing the page number with the name of the unit (e.g., "Igneous Rocks – 1," "Igneous Rocks – 2," "Igneous Rocks – A," "Igneous Rocks – B"), thus making reference to specific content or assignments easier for the teacher and students. Some teachers report that this sequencing design helps students align the notes they take with the specific lesson objectives and content being delivered.

Science teacher Kevin Broznik describes the numbered right-side pages of his students' notebooks as "teacher" or "input" pages, and the left-side numbered pages as "student work" or "output" pages. He finds this system helps students keep the new material that is presented by the teacher in the form of notes for the lesson content separate from their application or use. In his case, the interaction between the right and left side is visible to the students; they see what the teacher presented, and, on the other side, how they reorganized, revised, reproduced, or responded to the new content. This separation of notebook entries allows a student to quickly access the teacher-delivered content and the associated assignment work—feedback that supports better learning.

Some teachers find simple sequential numbering to be the best for their class content. The rationale is that student handwriting can vary widely, so some students need more pages than others to take notes. When students number the pages in their notebooks, it emphasizes that notebooks are a work in progress that will become a complete "volume" at the conclusion of the semester or school year.

A Table of Contents

As most students are familiar with structures and headings of informational texts, many teachers ask students to reserve the first several pages of their notebooks for an ongoing, developing table of contents. Figure 3.1 on page 62 shows an interactive notebook table of contents created by a student in math teacher Brad Tate's class. As this figure shows, the table of contents can be both a functional tool for finding material and a quick overview of the topics addressed in the course.

Even the younger students can create a table of contents without too much difficulty, and seeing their work presented in a structure parallel to what they have seen in books in their classroom, in a library, or at a bookstore makes their work feel more significant to them.

Teachers tell us that devoting class time to teaching notebook organizational techniques, such as page numbering, creating a table of contents, and ways to categorize separate units of study, reminds them to set aside regular and frequent class time for students to "keep their notebooks up-to-date" and interact with lesson material and notes. Furthermore, when all the notebooks in a class are organized in a similar way, teachers may scan students' work more easily and use the lesson-specific evidence of student understanding they find there as feedback to inform instructional adjustments, either on the spot or for a subsequent lesson.

FIGURE 3.1

Sample IN9 Table of Contents

TABLE of Contents — NOTES

PAGE #	PAGE TITLE	DATE ADDED
1	Real #'s and ab's value	8-18-10
2	Integers	8-23-10
3	Fractions on Calc	8-26-10
4	Mixed Numbers	8-27-10
5	Properties	8-30-10
6	Distributive Property	8-31-10
7	Order of Operations	8-31-10
8	Factors and Divisibility	9-2-10
9	Greatest Common Factor / Least Common Multiple	9-7-10
10	Variables, Expressions, and Equations	9-8-10
11	Partnering in Number Sequences	9-9-10
12	The Pythagorean Theorem	9-19-10
13	Perimeter	9-16-10
14	Area of Parallelograms	9-16-10
15	Area of Triangles	9-17-10
16	Area of Circles	9-20-10
17	Circumfrence of Circles	9-21-10

Courtesy of Brad Tate

Specialized Pages

After the initial setup, teachers may guide students to use specific types of pages for vocabulary words, assignments, progress tracking, and other specialized purposes. History teacher Dan Young says, "I have the students designate 'V' (vocabulary) next to the number on the top of the pages so the vocabulary 'journal' pages are easy to find when flipping through the notebooks." Elementary teachers do the same—marking a "V" designation on folders that young students use to store their vocabulary lists and related vocabulary activities.

Biology teacher Laura Turner asks her students to create an assignment index to keep track of the points earned on individual assignments (see Figure 3.2 on p. 64). Many art and technical education teachers favor special pages for step-by-step techniques that students will need to refer to during the coverage of multiple units, and English teachers who use a standard rubric for evaluating student writing throughout a term might have students set it up as a specialized page.

✠ Time to Reflect ✠

What specialized notebook pages would be helpful for the content area or age group you teach?

The GANAG-Structured Lesson and IN9s

As we have noted, what distinguishes the IN9s from other kinds of interactive notebooks are (1) the way in which they guide students to use high-yield strategies that complement lessons planned and delivered in accordance with the GANAG structure, and (2) the way in which their use supports formative assessment and guides the instructive feedback formative assessment generates. The skill of seeking and using feedback, while important for all learners, is one that academically at-risk learners definitely benefit from practicing daily. When students keep IN9s, both they and the teacher have a visible record of their evolving understanding, developing thinking skills, and the progress they are making toward the curriculum goals.

FIGURE 3.2
Sample IN9 Assignment Index

Assignment Index

Unit Name Cellular Reproduction . Unit # ___7___

Date	Assignment	Points Earned	Total Points
1-27-11	Study Guide 9.1 and 9.2	34	34
1-27-11	page 243 Foldable	5	5
1-28-11	Concept Map for Chap 9 (WEB)	5	5
1-31-11	9.1, 9.2, 9.3 Quiz	34	42
2-3-11	Unit 7 Test	90	100
2-16-11	Study Guide 9.1 and 9.2	29	29
2-18-11	DNA MODEL	50	55
2-23-11	Science Notebook 12-3	15	15
3-1-11	Study Guide 12-3	13	13
3-2-11	Transcription/Translation Flipbook	15	15
3-3-11	Unit 8 Review (Pink Review)	25	25
3-3-11	Unit 8 Test (DNA Test)	98	100
3-11-11	Genetics Quiz	25	30
3-15-11	Monohybrid Cross Practice Worksheet	12	15

Courtesy of Laura Turner

Throughout the next discussion, we highlight possible pairings between GANAG stages and high-yield strategies—pairings that many teachers have found effective in supporting the organization and flow of students' IN9s. For clarity, we refer to the strategies suggested for each stage of GANAG as "associated high-yield strategies"—those that help successful students stay successful and help struggling students become successful.

G – Setting a Goal: An Invitation to Join the Class

Associated High-Yield Strategies: Setting Objectives and Providing Feedback; Recognizing Effort and Providing Recognition; Collaborative Learning

Patty Grossman, a high school teacher, begins every class by presenting the first "G" of GANAG—the lesson goals provided by the curriculum document—which she projects on the board. Her students begin the class by turning to the page in their interactive notebooks in which they have stapled the unit's objective score sheet (OSS) (see Figure 3.3 on p. 66). The OSS provides a place for them to interact with goals and objectives on a lesson-by-lesson basis and track their progress toward achievement.

On the right side of the OSS, students use a common numerical scale to score themselves on the effort they plan to put into the lesson—a strategy employed to engage students in metacognition. Then, each student self-assesses, recording a score that reflects his or her pre-lesson knowledge of the objective's content. At the end of the lesson, the student self-assesses both his or her new level of understanding or ability as well as the effort invested in the learning. In this way, an OSS like the one in Figure 3.3 serves as a tracking sheet to document activity, effort, and results; it is similar to a tracking sheet one might use in an exercise program or a nutrition plan. Note, too, that a teacher might partially prepare an OSS for students who need extra time or assistance writing the goal statements.

Let's return to Patty's class. When the bell rings, students consider the lesson goal they see on the board and fill out their objective score sheets, sometimes sharing comments with a table partner. Within a couple of minutes, all are ready to learn, with their notebooks open. Patty says that it took a few weeks for her to remember and get used to the process, but it only took her students a day. She is

FIGURE 3.3

Template for a Secondary-Level OSS

Name _____ Block _____

Overall personal goal for this section:

_____

Plan for achieving this goal:

_____

	Effort Rubric
4	• Worked until completed • Pushed myself to continue • Viewed difficulties as opportunities to learn
3	• Worked until completed • Pushed myself to continue
2	• Some effort, but stopped when it became difficult
1	• Very little effort

	Understanding Rubric
4	• Got it and know how to use it in other ways
3	• Got it
2	• Some understanding; still have questions
1	• Still do not understand

Date	Text Section	Goal/Objectives	EFFORT (Rate 1–4)		UNDERSTANDING (Rate 1–4)	
			Before	After	Before	After

pleased with the routine that this specific attention to the goals creates both for her and for her students. It has increased attentiveness and has created the necessary rudder that many of her students need to navigate the transition between subjects and classes. Patty also tells a story about one of her students who asked for some extra copies of the OSS. When she asked why, he said he wanted to use them for his other classes, where the score sheets were not required.

For her 2nd graders, Stephanie Lane uses an OSS layout with less text but comparable value in self-assessment and self-reporting (see Figure 3.4 on p. 68). She observes that students are enthusiastic about keeping track of their work, and they love to show their progress to others. Stephanie comments that because they keep track of their own progress by the content objectives, they are more likely to speak up throughout the day about lingering questions they have. She adds that her parent-teacher conferences have been transformed by her ability to share objective score sheets—visual representations of student learning data—with parents and guardians.

Science teacher Lena Joch made a slight variation in her OSS format to address one of the curriculum keystones in their program—essential questions (see Figure 3.5 on p. 69). And technology specialist Diane Quirk suggests that teachers consider using an electronic OSS that includes an entry form and outputs data to a spreadsheet document (see Figures 3.6 and 3.7 on pp. 70–71).

Regardless of the objective score sheet's format, level of complexity, and degree of detail, its purpose is essentially the same. With regular use over a few days or weeks, an individual student will be able to see patterns of performance— data that can serve as a cue for when to seek help from the teacher (expert feedback) or peers (clarification feedback).

The OSS becomes a means to helping academically at-risk students self-regulate their learning behaviors and build positive habits. It also opens communication that can forge a stronger relationship between teacher and student about academic or nonacademic expectations, provides concrete evidence of learning that can be shown at home, and often leads to tangible improvement— not just in learning outcomes but also in students' attitudes toward learning. In short, working an OSS into lessons and students' interactive notebooks is a simple way to help mind achievement gaps.

FIGURE 3.4

Template for an Elementary-Level OSS

	Monday	Tuesday	Wednesday	Thursday	Friday
Math	We are learning about Before: 1 2 3 4 After: 1 2 3 4	We are learning about Before: 1 2 3 4 After: 1 2 3 4	We are learning about Before: 1 2 3 4 After: 1 2 3 4	We are learning about Before: 1 2 3 4 After: 1 2 3 4	We are learning about Before: 1 2 3 4 After: 1 2 3 4
Reading	We are learning about Before: 1 2 3 4 After: 1 2 3 4	We are learning about Before: 1 2 3 4 After: 1 2 3 4	We are learning about Before: 1 2 3 4 After: 1 2 3 4	We are learning about Before: 1 2 3 4 After: 1 2 3 4	We are learning about Before: 1 2 3 4 After: 1 2 3 4
Science S.S.	We are learning about Before: 1 2 3 4 After: 1 2 3 4	We are learning about Before: 1 2 3 4 After: 1 2 3 4	We are learning about Before: 1 2 3 4 After: 1 2 3 4	We are learning about Before: 1 2 3 4 After: 1 2 3 4	We are learning about Before: 1 2 3 4 After: 1 2 3 4
Word Study	We are learning about Before: 1 2 3 4 After: 1 2 3 4	We are learning about Before: 1 2 3 4 After: 1 2 3 4	We are learning about Before: 1 2 3 4 After: 1 2 3 4	We are learning about Before: 1 2 3 4 After: 1 2 3 4	We are learning about Before: 1 2 3 4 After: 1 2 3 4
Writing	We are learning about Before: 1 2 3 4 After: 1 2 3 4	We are learning about Before: 1 2 3 4 After: 1 2 3 4	We are learning about Before: 1 2 3 4 After: 1 2 3 4	We are learning about Before: 1 2 3 4 After: 1 2 3 4	We are learning about Before: 1 2 3 4 After: 1 2 3 4

Questions for My Teacher

1 = I do not know   2 = I know a little, but I still need to practice   3 = I know all about it and I'm ready for a test   4 = I know above and beyond!

Courtesy of Stephanie Lane

FIGURE 3.5
Template for an OSS Focused on Essential Questions

Name: _____ Subject: _____ Hour: _____

Unit: _____

My goal for this unit: _____

_____

Date	Essential Question	Objective(s)	Before-Class Understanding	After-Class Understanding
			4 3 2 1	4 3 2 1

Today, I learned . . .

Date	Essential Question	Objective(s)	Before-Class Understanding	After-Class Understanding
			4 3 2 1	4 3 2 1

Today, I learned . . .

Date	Essential Question	Objective(s)	Before-Class Understanding	After-Class Understanding
			4 3 2 1	4 3 2 1

Today, I learned . . .

Courtesy of Lena Joch

FIGURE 3.6

Sample Electronic OSS Entry Form

* Required

Date *

Text Section *

Objective/Goal for the Day *

Effort Rating (Pre:) *

1 2 3 4 5

○ ○ ○ ○ ○

Understanding before the lesson *

1 2 3 4 5

○ ○ ○ ○ ○

Understanding after the lesson *

1 2 3 4 5

○ ○ ○ ○ ○

Submit

Courtesy of Diane Quirk

The GANAG lesson structure calls for a teacher to direct the students back to the goal throughout the lesson, using regular goal-based feedback and a high-effect strategy such as collaborative learning (e.g., pair-sharing). The OSS provides a structured way for students to engage immediately in the lesson by writing down the goal, but the added elements of self-assessment and the monitoring of progress give the students and the teacher opportunities to recognize effort together or alone. For a reminder of the power of these

FIGURE 3.7

Sample Electronic OSS Spreadsheet Output

File   Edit   View   Insert   Format   Data   Tools   Form (1)   Help   Last edit was made 74 days ago by quirkytech

🖶 ↶ ↷ 🗋 ⋅ 🇹 $ % 123 ⋅   10pt ⧫   **B** Abc **A** ⋅ **A** ⋅ ⊞ ⋅   ≣ ⋅ ▦ ⋅   ≡ ⋅ Σ ⋅ 📊 ▽

fx │ Timestamp

	A	B	C	D	E	F	G
1	Timestamp	Date	Text Section	Objective/Goal for the Day	Effort Rating (Pre:)	Understanding before the lesson	Understanding after the lesson
2	7/31/2011 14:47:14	7/31/2011	Pgs 101-105	Goal 1	3	3	4
3							
4							
5							
6							

Courtesy of Diane Quirk

high-yield learning strategies, refer back to the effect sizes in Chapter 2, beginning on page 32.

There is great value in treating goal setting and performance tracking as both an individual and group activity. Ray Highway, a principal in a First Nations schools in northern Canada, shared a particularly compelling reason: "Since many of our dropouts have told us that they do not feel that they belong when they are in school, we see the act of writing down the goal as an invitation to join the class," Ray told us. "Self-assessing and sharing this information with the teacher and others is an act of courage, an act that confirms for the student that he or she belongs [to the class]."

⚛ Time to Reflect ⚛

How would you design an OSS for a group of students you teach?

A – Access Prior Knowledge: Fire Neurons

Associated High-Yield Strategies: Identify Similarities and Differences; Nonlinguistic Representations; Cooperative Learning; Use Questions, Cues, and Advance Organizers

With the OSS priming students for the lesson, the notebooks are open; students are ready to jot down thoughts or responses to a cue to access prior knowledge as a way to prepare to integrate the new knowledge they will encounter in the lesson. To build and activate prior knowledge, some teachers provide a cue using a picture, object, or some other nonlinguistic representation; other teachers ask a question to cue what students might know that is similar to or different from the new information. Often, accessing prior student knowledge can be done by analogy; the new information may truly be new to the students, but they may have background knowledge they can use to forge a connection or pathway between their own knowledge and the new concepts.

In Ron Hensley's math class, for example, he projected three pictures: a wheelchair ramp, a roof with shingles, and ski runs on a mountain. His students got to work in the left side of their notebooks, responding to Ron's directions to come up with a fourth object related to the math concept the pictures illustrated (slope) and then justify their picks. Students shared answers in pairs and then contributed ideas for whole-class consideration. Ron's purpose was to trigger students' ideas about slope as part of "everyday math," so he began the lesson by prompting them to connect the mathematical concept to concrete objects in the world around them.

In a counseling class, Alex DeMatteis used a demonstration at the beginning of a lesson by asking that a volunteer student fill a container with small, medium, and large stones, but first all students had to write down the order in which they would insert the various sizes of stones. As the students quickly recorded responses in the left side of their notebooks, Alex walked around, gazing over shoulders. Then Alex asked one student to demonstrate his container-filling method. As the boy did so, Alex talked about the connection between this activity and the need to prioritize during decision making. The different sizes of rocks, he explained, represented small, medium, and large problems. Now the students were ready to take notes on making good decisions.

Casually, we call the stage of accessing prior knowledge the time when students "fire their neurons" before they start forming new connections. For students to learn information effectively, they need to integrate or connect the new knowledge to their existing concepts and beliefs, which could be personal or subject-matter knowledge. One characteristic of all students, academically at risk or not, is that they have rich background experiences to share; they are often surprised at how much they can articulate or are able to share that connects them to the new topics.

There are at least three ways for students to connect to new material and record it in their notebooks:

1. Respond to a nonlinguistic representation (video clip, object, picture) by answering or generating a question.

2. Review notes from previous days and highlight key academic terms.

3. Complete a quiz or answer questions about a specific topic.

The different options allow students a wide variety of ways to connect, creating opportunities for students who otherwise might not have been ready to learn. We often refer to this step as one of "neuronal courtesy," because it helps every student make the necessary mental leap from the previous class to the present class. When asked to pair-share before providing responses to the whole group, students can fire one another's neurons.

When students are given directions to keep notebooks and set goals, this courteous step adds to the predictability of class for academically at-risk students. It gives them the opportunity to engage with a peer or connect to a visual representation, and it reinforces the idea that every lesson is an important part of the progression of learning.

✖ Time to Reflect ✖

How does asking students to document their responses to exercises that access their prior knowledge support engagement for otherwise disengaged learners?

N – New Information: The Information or Procedural Content of a Lesson

Associated High-Yield Strategies: Summarizing and Taking Notes; Homework and Practice; Cooperative Learning; Use Questions, Cues, and Advance Organizers

At this point in the lesson, students are ready to learn and take notes on the new information, either declarative knowledge (e.g., factual information presented in a science lesson or a textbook) or procedural knowledge (e.g., software formats presented in a business marketing class) that requires them to write or practice sequential steps.

Techniques for note taking vary depending on the subject matter. If one searches on the Internet, many study skill sites offer note-taking methods such as outlining, charting or mapping, two-column notes, or using index cards. Some formats include making pictorial or visual representations as well as recording text. Since verbatim transcription of what the teacher says is the least effective way to learn new information (Marzano et al., 2001), teachers are advised to teach students different ways to take notes, providing the guidance and time students need to become proficient at using various note-taking techniques.

An interesting alternative to traditional note taking for elementary students is teaching them to use "foldables" as a way to scaffold the learning process. A foldable, a three-dimensional graphic organizer, is simply any sheet of paper folded in various ways to organize pictures or words; Dinah Zike offers examples and resources online (www.dinah.com). After the students make their foldables or their version of notes, they can paste them into the appropriate places in their notebooks.

As indicated in the set-up discussion, some teachers direct students to reserve the right side of their notebook for recording information provided by the teacher (or acquired from a reading or other source) and use the left side of the notebook, the page opposite the new information, to reorganize this material after the fact, reflect on it, summarize it, or complete an assignment related to it. Information and reflections can be jotted down in words or pictographs. A glue stick or stapler comes in handy for assignments on worksheets; students can fold the worksheet in half and glue or staple it into their IN9.

Melanie Hansen teaches middle school English. For a declarative knowledge lesson about a novel, for example, she may deliver a lecture and ask her students to take notes on the right side of their notebook. She will pause periodically to allow students to check in with a partner, share understandings, and get clarification feedback before continuing. For a follow-up homework assignment, students might use the notes they took in order to create a graphic organizer overview of the content on the left side of their notebooks—perhaps a fish scale organizer or flowchart. For a procedural lesson like poetry writing, the students would take notes on what Melanie taught about poem structure on the right side of their notebooks, and then write their original poems on the left.

"Most of my 'unmotivated' students have the ability to learn new information," Melanie says, "but they had decided not to perform for some reason. Associating high-yield strategies to my lesson (GANAG) and their notebooks (IN9s) revolutionized my teaching, because now I deliberately model, pause, question, and wait for students to engage with the content, and I can see in every student's notebook how they are progressing. I feel like I have transformed my teaching, and I have fewer 'unmotivated' students than in all of the other years I've taught."

Tammy Riedel teaches Spanish and math. As she began to purposefully incorporate the high-yield strategies into her lessons and have students keep interactive notebooks, she realized that teaching students to cooperate by pair-sharing or shoulder-talks stimulated them to generate their own questions, further increasing their engagement. In the past, students who were not keeping up or had not done the problems seemed to accept that they were not going to be given extra time or correctives. Since they have begun using IN9s, Tammy's students are better prepared to look back through material and generate questions based on their work or what they see in others' notebooks. When her students became accustomed to looking at each other's work in their notebooks, they welcomed interacting with different students, simply because they came to realize that sharing their ideas and gleaning feedback from others could enhance their own learning.

Tammy also notes that walking around the room to see what her students write in their notebooks during a lesson and regularly collecting the notebooks for careful review give her a clear direction for reteaching individuals, groups, or the whole class.

Here, at the "N" stage of a lesson, teachers often set students to work on activities that involve working with a partner to share what they have written in their notebooks and to summarize that knowledge on a new page; after all, two heads can be better than one when it comes to understanding the new content or skills of a lesson more deeply. Many teachers observe that today's students—a generation raised with social networking and texting—tend to be more open to communicating with others. Class pairing directed toward clarifying new knowledge or information can become an extension of students' natural habits of sharing their thoughts. It also helps many students stay on task rather than disengaging. Not only does the expectation that they will work with a partner help to keep them working on a task they might otherwise ignore or abandon, but the opportunity to get clarifying feedback from a peer can help any student overcome obstacles that can make a task or topic seem overwhelming.

⚗ Time to Reflect ⚗

Which methods discussed in this section might engage your less-motivated students?

A – Application: Generating New Ideas and Shaping Procedures

Associated Strategies: Identifying Similarities and Differences; Generating and Testing Hypotheses; Asking Analytical Questions; Practice

This stage of a lesson prompts students to think about and use newly encountered declarative knowledge or practice the steps of procedural knowledge to gain skill proficiency. In this section, we will discuss these two types of knowledge separately.

Applying thinking skills to declarative knowledge. Students gain new declarative knowledge by engaging in activities such as taking notes during a lecture, participating in discussion, viewing a video, or reading. The application stage of a lesson is when they interact with that new information and apply thinking skills to make that information their own. In *Classroom Instruction That Works* (Marzano et al., 2001), Janie and her co-authors noted that research organizes thinking skills into three categories: (1) identifying similarities and differences, (2) generating and testing hypotheses, and (3) questioning. At this stage of the lesson, students may engage in any of these activities, capturing their work in their notebooks.

In a geology unit, for example, Gale Cameron and her students focus on the standard "Investigate fossils in sedimentary rock layers to gather evidence of changing life forms." After presenting new information about the characteristics of various kinds of fossils dated to different prehistoric eras, Gale launches an activity in which students look at a variety of fossil examples and compare them (identifying similarities and differences). Her instructions include asking them to copy the following list into their notebooks, which maps out the kind of thinking they need to do as well as how they will be approaching and using material from the "N" stage of the lesson:

1. Select items to compare.
2. Select characteristics on which to compare the items.
3. Identify what is similar and different about items based on characteristics.
4. Summarize or make a generalization about the topic.

The thinking or application part of a declarative knowledge lesson lends itself to collaboration and seeking new information in response to questions that arise. The students work through the steps, possibly creating a visual map in their notebooks to guide their thinking before they create a separate paper, electronic slide show, or other presentation of their application of their knowledge about the fossils.

Practicing the steps of procedural knowledge. When students learn procedural knowledge, the interactive notebooks provide a place to record the steps of the skill and document practice. Over a short period of time, students can create an impressive, and motivating, record of both work and progress.

Consistent use of IN9s helps make the content that students are asked to apply more readily available. Having content knowledge accessible in their notebooks makes it easier for students to engage in application activities, alone or in a group, because needed information is available and categorized uniformly by all students.

G – Goal Review: Self-Assessment and Self-Reporting

Associated High-Yield Strategies: Setting Objectives and Providing Feedback; Recognizing Effort

The end of a lesson too often sounds like a bell ringing and looks like students hurrying to pack up and head out the door. In GANAGed lessons, delivered in association with IN9s, the end of the lesson is a planned event. Anticipating the end of the lesson, the teacher cues students to return to the OSS to reassess their understanding of the content and the effort they invested while the teacher circulates to see how the students self-report.

Let's pause to reconsider the effect on learning of student self-reporting. Hattie (2009) confirms that students tend to provide very accurate pictures of their own levels of understanding and the effort they invest in the process of learning—in other words, they know what they know and don't know, and they know how hard they work. According to Hattie's research, when teachers set challenging goals and provide a way for students to see their progress in attaining those goals (such as using objective score sheets), student confidence and achievement rise.

Another recommended high-yield strategy to use at the end of the lesson is summarizing. Teachers might, for example, cue students to respond to a summarizing prompt, draw a stoplight to indicate progress, or spontaneously create a pithy "bumper sticker" to show their understanding of or questions about the objectives of the lesson. When students write their responses in their notebooks, these responses are then readily available for starting the next class. Students can flip back to this "generalization" of the lesson's learning when they are asked to access prior knowledge at the beginning of the next lesson. Making generalizations about lesson content (or what we call "putting a tab on the folder") and recording these generalizations in IN9s allows teachers to see how well students have understood and where additional review may be helpful.

✂ Time to Reflect ✂

How do you see the end of a lesson serving as a significant part of goal-related feedback important to at-risk learners?

Learning Is Marginalized by Poverty

Linda Mishkin, who spent 30 years as a teacher in private schools, now teaches in a public high school in the South Bronx in New York. She notes that urban high schools bleed students every year. Students show up to start the new school year, but absenteeism slowly erodes their performance and chance for school success. According to Linda, "Some of the absenteeism is clearly attributable to their lives outside of school, but I'm also sure that some could be mitigated if we paid attention to what students say about class itself and paid closer attention to what they are doing while they are supposed to be learning."

Linda's point is a critical one. Factors outside school, and outside educators' control, certainly have an effect on student success, but we can rise to the challenge of helping our students learn more effectively while they are in school.

One of the characteristics often associated with students whose academically at-risk status places them at risk of dropping out is low socioeconomic status—poverty. While it might seem strange to come this far in a book about addressing achievement gaps, and in a chapter about reaching students who are academically at risk, without mentioning children who grow up in poverty, we believe that teachers can mitigate many out-of-school factors that potentially affect students and their learning by changing intentional teaching habits. Thus, we have focused on a solution-based approach to helping students rather than on factors that are beyond a teacher's control, such as poverty.

Ruby Payne (2005) has dedicated her career to building awareness about how to successfully teach children who are otherwise considered low functioning. Payne cites Reuven Feuerstein's work on mediation, noting that children in poverty who do not learn and do not regularly use skills like planning, predicting, negotiating cause and effect, appreciating the importance of consequences, and controlling impulsivity in their lives outside school not only may lack proficiency with these skills, which are critical to academic success, but also may be unlikely to understand why these skills are so highly valued by their teachers. Skill disadvantages are compounded by this sense of disconnection, and these students find themselves bored, unmotivated, and easily distracted in the classroom.

To help students whose learning is marginalized by poverty apply their great learning potential, it is important that a classroom be the place where, for five to six hours every day, teachers teach strategies and provide multiple opportunities for these students to seek the feedback about progress that will help them develop and nurture high-effect learning skills. The IN9 is a valuable tool in this effort. Its use helps students become better planners and predictors by engaging them in regular goal setting and self-assessment. And IN9 use, with its emphasis on soliciting and providing thoughtful feedback and its structured processes, helps nurture thoughtfulness, reflection, metacognition, collaboration, and impulse control—all valuable tools for success inside and outside school.

We are inspired, although maybe a bit haunted, by Ronald Edmonds's observation from the late 1970s as he advocated that all students should have the opportunity to attend effective schools:

> It seems to me:
> a. We can, whenever and wherever we choose, successfully teach all children whose schooling is of interest to us;
> b. We already know more than we need to do that; and
> c. Whether or not we do it must finally depend on how we feel about the fact that we haven't so far. (Edmonds, 1979, p. 23)

In summary, using IN9s benefits academically at-risk students in the following ways:

- IN9s help to develop organizational skills.
- IN9s promote assignment completion by linking assignments to achieving learning goals.
- IN9s provide a daily, personalized map of the content and skills learned.
- IN9s ensure that students are prepared to share work in cooperative learning groups.
- IN9s provide more evidence of learning progress to improve students' communication with teachers and teachers' communication with parents.

- IN9s support frequent, immediate feedback keyed to specific parts of lessons and specific assignments.

Teaching students to create and use IN9s is a simple, practical, and effective way to support every student in any classroom.

Renewing Enthusiasm for Teaching *and* Learning

Rewards that can go a long way toward regenerating teachers' enthusiasm for their profession happen when academically at-risk learners want to come to school, show interest in learning, and make a turnaround in their achievement progress. Even though these rewards are the ones that can truly make a teacher's day, week, or year, they are owned by students, and they can be life changing for youth, changing directions in their attitude, confidence, and demonstrated potentials. Interactive notebooks that incorporate GANAG and the nine high-yield strategies are perhaps the most powerful tools for teachers and students in ensuring that learning rewards are experienced. Renewed excitement in learning is being shown through the use of these notebooks—excitement that is translating to the minding and closing of achievement gaps among academically at-risk students.

Educator Voice

Jenn Sykora, High School Spanish and Health Teacher

For Jenn Sykora, a self-confessed "overachiever," it always seemed that bright students who underachieved in school had mostly themselves to blame. Certainly her teaching couldn't play a part in their failure—or could it? Here, Jenn talks about the epiphany that upended her long-standing beliefs and about how helping students organize and engage with their learning in interactive notebooks has given her a new outlook on what is possible.

Where I'm Coming From

My brother, Michael, is three years younger than I, and he struggled in school. Michael didn't complete assignments. He turned work in late, took few notes, and rarely studied.

I, on the other hand, was good at "going to school." Teachers loved having me in class. A traditional overachiever, I always took meticulous notes, listened intently to every word that left a teacher's mouth, completed assignments promptly, and studied for every quiz and test. My classes were at advanced levels, so I was surrounded by other students who were equally academically successful.

One weekend when I was home from college, Michael was struggling with an English assignment given by a teacher I'd had a few years earlier. I offered to help him, even as I was chiding him for not having put in the proper effort. Although I say I "helped" him, I basically redid the entire assignment. All week I waited anxiously for the teacher to return my brother's assignment. I was expecting an *A;* instead, the assignment was returned with a note that read, "Michael, this looks like your sister's work. Please redo."

So much for helping.

A few years later, right out of college and still working on my master's degree, I was hired at an all-boys high school. As a novice teacher, I found myself asking, "Why can't my students stay organized? Why don't they take good notes? Why don't they do homework? Why don't they study?" My classroom was full of students just like Michael, and I tried my best to help them, with very inconsistent results. If only they would "do school" the way I had done it! But they *didn't,* and to my great frustration, it seemed like they *wouldn't.* It was clear to me that the *D*s and *F*s my students earned were due to their own lack of effort.

My *Aha!* Moment

I tend be skeptical of professional development for teachers. Although many of the ideas presented in PD sessions are clearly worthy, implementing them in my own classroom seldom makes much difference for the group of students who really need to improve. For years, the post-PD pattern was the same: I'd try new ways for a while, but at the end of the quarter, I would still have the same breakout of overachievers and underachievers.

That pattern changed with the introduction of GANAG. I remember Janie Pollock asking about the progress-report conferences we had with our students' parents. She wanted to know if we ever sat down with the parents and talked about what their child did not do: "Your son doesn't do homework. Your daughter doesn't turn her work in on time. Your son doesn't take notes. . . ."

I nodded my head in agreement. *Finally,* I thought, *we're about to hear professional development ideas related to the type of students I deal with in my classroom.* So I was startled and dumbfounded by what Janie said next: "The problem is probably not the student. The problem just might be the teacher."

What? Had I heard her correctly? How insulting! She had never observed my class, yet she had the audacity to suggest I was to blame for the students who fail my class. I continued to sit and listen, but only because I had to, and because I'll always be too much of an overachiever to ever tune out entirely. And as Janie continued to speak, I began to see the reasonableness of her ideas. What's more, she had the pedagogical research to back them up.

With the encouragement and support of our administration and Janie, our staff began implementing research on learning in our classrooms. One such strategy was the use of interactive student notebooks. It has changed the way I educate my students, and it has transformed not just my classroom but many classrooms in my school.

Organization

Now, back to my brother. Organization was never Michael's strength. When he had a homework assignment, he rarely had the resources necessary to complete it, and when it was time to study for a test, he did not know what to study. I encountered plenty of unorganized students like Michael during my first few years of teaching. Many could not keep track of a vocabulary list or a set of notes from one class to the next. Others took notes but were unable to find what they needed in their notebook. Organization is a teachable skill, yet with so much to cover in class, I was more inclined to provide students with additional copies of whatever they had misplaced, enabling unorganized habits rather than addressing them.

Interactive notebooks have minimized the problems related to organization. My students keep all important resources for my class in one place now—their IN9s. This is especially crucial for "building block" courses, like math and Spanish, in which students must constantly expand on knowledge gained in previous lessons. The well-executed IN9 includes a table of contents, which directs students to the page where they can find lesson information, clearly labeled or even highlighted. In each lesson's section, they can find not just facts and procedural steps but work that requires the meaningful application of both.

The clear structure of an interactive notebook helps students establish solid organizational habits quickly. By the end of the first quarter, I no longer need to direct my students to complete their notes on the right side of their notebook, write the lesson title or date at the top of the page, or keep their table of contents current. They have developed automatic habits of keeping their notebooks organized without direction from me, and it is now easier for them to find information that will answer a question they have or enable them to help a classmate who needs assistance. Whether completing an assignment in or out of class, if they have their notebook, they have the resources they need.

My students appreciate having a resource that maximizes their success in my class and provides them with strategies they are able to utilize in other classes and in their postsecondary endeavors. While the IN9 has introduced techniques to help the already-organized students improve, it has also given the "Michaels" who lacked organization a way to attain those skills.

Student Engagement

Use of interactive notebooks has increased the engagement of all my students, overachievers and "Michaels" alike. My lessons are aligned with the GANAG format and structured so that students work in their notebooks throughout a lesson. In effect, the focus in my classroom has shifted from teaching to learning. Students are actively engaged with concepts through activities that promote their learning. In both my Spanish and health classes, students write each lesson's goal (G) on the objective score sheet in their IN9, which is one factor that sets the IN9 strategy apart from traditional note taking. Interaction with the goal enhances the lesson for the students and provides a clear learning target to which students can assess their understanding and track their progress. When I ask students to use the notebook during activities that help them access prior knowledge (A), the curiosity generated and the prior learning they recall are captured on the page for them to refer to and for me to see as a I walk around. My students always use their IN9s to gather new information or lay out the steps to a new skill or process (N). They know that this material is the foundation for subsequent activities in which they will apply (A) their new knowledge or skill in a meaningful way. And then, at the end of the lesson, we return to the lesson's goals (G) by revisting the objective score sheet, a tool students use to solidify their learning and self-assess their understanding and the effort they've invested. Incorporating the objective score sheet into the IN9 at both the beginning and end of the lesson is essential, because it enables students to monitor their progress daily and over the course of a unit. Furthermore, students want to award themselves high scores, so they are more motivated to make an effort and participate in lesson activities. Prior to the summative assessment, each student knows whether or not he has mastered the material based on his attainment of the goals throughout the unit.

Since the implementation of the IN9 in my classroom, I have never been asked, "Why are we doing this?" Now my students know that all activities within a lesson help them construct meaning and achieve the goal established at the beginning of each lesson. They can see the relevance of the work we're doing together.

Comprehension

Common sense tells us that engagement is likely to lead to comprehension. Students gain understanding from lessons in which they are active learners. And their learning, documented in their IN9s, certainly is active. My students' notebooks are full of diagrams, visuals, and charts that record and support their learning experience. Rather than "give knowledge," I now facilitate learning through the goals I set and share, the information I provide, the tasks I set, and the guidance and opportunities for feedback I offer.

Because note taking is one of the nine research-based strategies proven to maximize student understanding and help students retain information for extended periods of time, it is only fitting that the IN9 promotes the effectiveness of those strategies. Of course, note taking is not the only high-yield strategy that naturally lends itself to the IN9. The rest of the nine high-yield strategies—identifying similarities and differences; reinforcing effort; practice; nonlinguistic representations; setting objectives; generating and testing hypothesis; and questions, cues, and advance organizers—are all easily and regularly integrated into IN9 work. The notebook also helps students recognize and build connections between the information and application components of a lesson. They collect new information on the right side of the notebook and apply the new information on the left, which further promotes the relationship between knowledge gathered from various sources and ways they can use that knowledge in daily life. Students at all academic levels master material more readily and perform better on assessments.

In Conclusion

Reflecting back on the incident in which I completed my brother's assignment, I wonder if he would have needed my help if his teacher had been using interactive notebooks. My guess is an emphatic no. Had that been the case, he would have had the resources to guide him in achieving the task, and he would have been engaged in class, which would have given him a better understanding of the material.

Ten years ago, I would have said that my underachieving brother was responsible for his classroom failure. Today, with the help of interactive notebooks, GANAG, and high-yield instructional strategies, I believe it's possible to transform my "Michaels" into organized and engaged master learners. *All* my students can attain the title "achiever" if *I* provide them with the tools for success . . . if *I* make a few simple changes and improvements in my practice.

4

English Language Learners: Incorporating Language Standards as Goals

WHEN ILEANA DAVIS, AN ELEMENTARY SCHOOL ENGLISH LANGUAGE teacher, attended a required training session focused on lesson planning, she did not expect that she was about to have "a moment"—a great epiphany that would change the way she thought about herself as a teacher and the way she thought about how students learn.

Generally speaking, Ileana often struggled to connect the topics addressed in professional development sessions to her specific situation: teaching eight daily sessions of English language instruction, half of which are inclusion and half of which are pull-out. During this particular professional development session, when Ileana heard a comment about the importance of teaching students to interact with and track progress toward content goals and objectives, she shrugged; she and her colleagues had been doing that for a long time. But then Ileana heard about an application of the concept she had never even considered: teaching English language learners (ELLs) to interact with and track their progress toward *language learning* goals and objectives. The moment occurred. The light bulb turned on.

"What a simple, obvious statement, and yet it seemed entirely new to me," Ileana tells us. "As the EL teacher in my building, for the past three years, my focus had been on making sure my EL students were learning the content.

My job was literally to prepare them for the state benchmark tests because my students were the 'make-it-or-break-it' group for our school to make the Adequate Yearly Progress goal. Nobody had ever said anything about tracking student progress toward the language goals, and certainly, nobody had suggested that the ELLs could track that progress themselves!"

This realization set Ileana, a National Board Certified Teacher of English as a New Language, on a new path—one that included providing her students with clear language learning goals in addition to content goals, and success criteria for both. Ileana noted that there seemed to be a somersault question here: if the general education teacher taught content and she, the EL specialist, *also* taught content, then who taught the language? ELLs' academic achievement improves as their English proficiency improves. Unless somebody takes deliberate, goal-focused action to improve English proficiency, language learning can stall, and these students can too easily remain where they often are—in the gap. Gersten and Baker (2000) came to the same conclusion: "We encourage researchers and educators to consider *language learning* and *content-area learning* as distinct educational goals rather than assuming that increased use of oral language in school will automatically lead to increased academic learning and the development of higher-order thinking skills" (p. 460).

Ileana says that the solutions she uses today had been *invisible in plain sight*. English language standards are available; however, most teachers have not used them in formative assessment for language learning or to teach students self-monitoring. Ileana laughs at the idea of being "a deviant," clarifying that the "positive deviant" student and teacher behavior is a deliberate, focused approach on improving language learning not *in lieu of* a focus on improving content learning but *in concert with* it. Once Ileana and her colleagues learned how to use the language goals, both in inclusion classrooms as well as in pull-out situations, they began to see ways to mind the language gap in their classrooms. Setting clear, distinct language goals is definitely a beginning.

This chapter is directed toward both classroom teachers and specialists who work with ELLs. It builds on the tenets described in Chapter 1—teachers intentionally changing their teaching habits to incorporate the following practices:

1. Deliberately providing learning goals (here, for language as well as for content).

2. Teaching students to interact with these goals by tracking their own progress.

3. Purposefully using and directing students to use high-yield learning strategies to maximize formative feedback and further achievement.

Language Goals and Content Goals: Separate but Coordinated

As we have explained, a good lesson begins with the teacher stating the goal or objective—the first "G" in the GANAG structure. Yet both EL specialist teachers and general education teachers express confusion about how to set lesson goals for their English language learners. The two questions they tend to ask us are "Should I set a separate language goal for ELLs to accompany the lesson's content goal?" and "Should my ELLs pursue the same content goals that my general education students do?" The answers here are yes and yes.

It is important to note that language learning does support content learning. However, assuming this happens automatically—or even assuming that language learning is dependably automatic, something that students pick up with five or six hours of EL support a week—rather than taking deliberate action to make it happen contributes to the persistence of learning gaps. While the task of determining and using two sets of standards may sound a bit overwhelming, teachers can draw on both district-adopted language standards and curriculum content goals provided by the state—or now, the Common Core State Standards.

For some teachers, what gives them pause is not the idea of extra work but that setting separate language and content goals seems at odds with the philosophy of inclusion, which champions integrating content and language objectives and mainstreaming students with special needs. Prior to the 1990s, English language learners were primarily taught in resource rooms, receiving language instruction and much subject-area instruction in pull-out programs. Research since has confirmed that all students benefit from the less restrictive education environment that inclusion offers, but the widespread belief in integrating special needs students into general education classes for most of their coursework does not prevent many general classroom teachers from feeling uncertain about how best to meet these students' needs, especially in schools when time with the EL specialist is limited.

We believe the following to be the best course of action for these teachers:

- Set content goals (CGs) and language goals (LGs) separately in every lesson.
- Provide a way for ELLs to self-assess on both CGs and LGs.
- Provide a way to track and generate feedback relative to ELLs' daily progress on both language learning goals and content goals (in collaboration with the EL teacher, as needed).
- Engage ELLs in high-yield strategies that increase their interaction with both language and content learning.

Sources for Language Goals

The idea of setting separate language learning goals for lessons is a lot less daunting when you consider that there are plenty available to choose from, all generally describing proficiency levels using numbers and developmental terms such as "1" (beginning), "2" (intermediate), and "3" (fluent). The reauthorized Elementary and Secondary Education Act, more familiarly known as the No Child Left Behind Act of 2001, requires all states to provide language learning standards; some states have developed their own, while others have adopted standards from outside providers. A number of school districts have carefully aligned their state language standards with the Common Core State Standards, meaning that teachers are easily able to find both content and language learning standards in district curriculum documents.

Many states post their language standards alongside other subject-area standards on their websites. For example:

- Arkansas provides a framework of both language learning standards and subject-specific standards, designed to be "congruent and progressive from grade level to grade level." Both sets of standards are available in various formats to encourage use (www.arkansased.org/educators/curriculum/frameworks.html).

• Washington state English Language Development Standards address "four proficiency levels (beginning/advanced beginning, intermediate, advanced, and transitional) in each of the four language domains of Listening, Speaking, Reading, and Writing. A fifth domain, Comprehension, is embedded within the domains of Listening and Reading" (www.k12.wa.us/migrant bilingual/eld.aspx).

• Many states have adopted the World-Class Instructional Design and Assessment (WIDA) English Language Proficiency Standards and its companion English Language Proficiency Test (www.wida.us/standards). WIDA provides standards in a comprehensive framework that blends language levels with clustered grade-level content area and social interaction topics, but it also provides "Can-Do Descriptors for Listening, Reading, Writing, and Speaking," an abridged but very explicit set of graduated standards appropriate for emerging to fluent language learners.

In short, setting language goals and content goals within a lesson while maintaining a relationship between them allows ELLs to receive more specific and timely feedback as they progress in listening, speaking, reading, and writing English. Jana Echevarria (2006), co-developer of the Sheltered Instruction Observation Protocol (SIOP), puts it this way: "The language objective ensures that necessary English language development is not overlooked and that some aspect of language is practiced daily" (p. 20). Creating separate-but-linked language goals and content goals helps to eliminate the ambiguity that can derail learning; students can clearly see their intended learning goal in reading, writing, listening, and speaking as it applies to the content area goals and objectives. Figure 4.1 shows some examples—language goals paired with content goals in the context of different subject-area lessons designed for different grade levels and language proficiency levels. The sample content and language goals in this figure (drawn from various classroom and literature sources, including an early draft of the English Language Development Standards for the State of Colorado) illustrate how the two types of goals can be combined in daily lessons.

	FIGURE 4.1	
	Sample Coordinated Content Goals and Language Goals	
Subject	**Lesson Content Goals (CG)**	**Lesson Language Goals (LG)**
Elementary art	Describe subject matter in art (landscapes, still life).	*Listening (beginning):* Demonstrate comprehension of . . . information by responding nonverbally (e.g., listening, pointing, moving, matching, drawing, or gesturing, or with simple word responses). *Speaking (beginning):* Use both social and academic learned vocabulary in context.
Middle school science	Determine the pH value of different liquids and use information to discuss related safety and dangers.	*Writing (intermediate):* Record and organize classroom procedures (e.g., science experiments, math problem solving, directions). *Speaking (beginning):* Respond to simple questions related to immediate context with single words or phrases.
Middle school humanities	Explain how the Greeks and Romans used myths to answer the eight fundamental questions in their societies. Understand the philosophical assumptions and basic beliefs underlying an author's work.	*Reading (advanced):* Apply reading strategies to understand more complex text and unfamiliar words (e.g., decoding, previewing, skimming/scanning, problem solving, word attack skills, prior knowledge).
High school history	Understand the link between the Scientific Revolution and the Age of Enlightenment through the ideas, individuals, and beliefs that emerged in European society.	*Writing (intermediate):* Describe characters (persons) and settings and summarize events. *Reading (intermediate):* Understand and analyze text for literal and implied meaning.

✻ Time to Reflect ✻

How might your teaching practices change if you provide separate language and content goals for ELL students? What benefits do you see resulting for the students?

Standards documents, like those we have listed in this section, give any teacher or specialist access to professionally developed language goals to include in the first "G" in a GANAG lesson. The GANAG approach, encouraging deliberate student interaction with goals at the beginning and end of every lesson and regular opportunities for goal-focused feedback throughout, is as effective for language learning as it is for content learning. In both cases, the outcomes are substantial gains in students' engagement, achievement, and overall confidence.

✻ Time to Reflect ✻

How familiar are you with your state's English language learning standards? What challenges and benefits do you see relative to incorporating these standards into your lesson design?

One Teacher's Before and After

Ileana Davis, the teacher introduced at the beginning of this chapter, acknowledges that her district had provided her with a good starting point. To begin with, all of her district's English language learners had been tested and placed into levels, meaning that teachers and specialists were aware of their students' language proficiency levels. In addition, teachers had ready access to the state English language learning frameworks that showed all levels of language proficiency standards written as goals—a familiar format comparable to the general education standards and benchmarks.

Ileana also had at her disposal two district-developed documents that her department considered critical: a checklist of language skills that teachers completed when they recommended a student for a proficiency-level change and a similar checklist attached to the report card. Both captured good information, but neither was sufficient to provide frequent, formative feedback that could guide language development on a lesson-by-lesson basis. What she and her students needed were new tools.

Progressing with a new language was like progressing with a sport, Ileana reasoned. When she played softball in college, it was the combination of daily practice and frequent, skill-specific guidance from her coach and teammates that helped her become a better player. She remembered how getting new insight about what she was doing on the field or new information about what she might do differently in the batter's box helped her improve and motivated her to set more challenging goals. As soon as Ileana retooled her assessment checklists into student self-assessment forms, or objective score sheets, and teacher goal-tracking forms, she was well on her way to transforming her students' language development. Figure 4.2 (see p. 96) shows Ileana's observation of how GANAGing both content and lesson goals and using these two forms changed her approach and improved student performance.

For most teachers, being able to retool an existing resource saves time and also contributes to successfully changing habits. Checklists are familiar to EL teachers, and increased effectiveness is just a matter of learning to use them a bit differently, as Ileana did.

Student Self-Assessment

In Chapter 3, we described how using an objective score sheet provides a way for students to self-assess: to interact with content goals and be more actively aware of their progress. An OSS is just as effective for students pursuing language goals, and it can be tailored to varying language proficiencies and to elementary and secondary learners. The objective score sheet for a language goal can be used right alongside any OSS used for content goals. Figure 4.3 (see p. 97) shows an example—a student-friendly and ELL-friendly document that Ileana designed for her 1st graders at the second level of proficiency.

FIGURE 4.2

One EL Teacher's Thoughts on the "Before and After" of Integrated Content and Language Goals

---

Teacher's Goal: Monitor Students' Language-Skill Progress

I used to ...	But now I ...	Comments and Questions
Focus on the content standards. My instruction was informed by test data: the content standards that my ELL students fell short of on quarterly assessments. My main priority was to get my students ready for state testing—which is a big factor in making AYP.	*Focus on the language skills.* I focus more on the fundamentals of the language standards—the building blocks of language my students need in order to be able to interact and understand the content better each day. My instructional guidance comes from the daily data on my tracking sheet; they reveal the skills students are struggling with and signal me to provide more instruction or reteach.	I am constantly rethinking and changing my tracking sheets as needed. Eventually, I want to expand my tracking sheets to use with all my grade-level groups. I do continue to teach to the content standards, but I have expanded my focus to address both.

Teacher's Goal: Help Students Monitor Their Own Language-Skill Progress

I used to ...	But now I ...	Comments and Questions
Review the objectives with the students. My EL training directed me to do this, so I did, but I never thought to have students interact with the goals. I knew what activities I wanted students to complete by the end of the week, but my students did not have the chance to share their perceptions or their learning. I could never be sure if my students had really understood the concept or not, because I did not ask them directly.	*Find out how my students feel about learning each language skill.* By drawing simple "expression faces" associated with specific skills, my students show me every day if they are feeling more confident or needing my help. I am now able to provide immediate, one-on-one assistance and timely course correction rather than finding out weeks down the road that they did not "get it."	I am working to make the OSS/goal sheets more individualized. I need those students to have a goal sheet that is more representative of where they are in comparison to the group as a whole; that way, if I must move forward on a skill for the sake of the group, any student who is not yet ready to move on will still have her/his goals from the previous skills.

Courtesy of Ileana Davis

FIGURE 4.3

Sample Language Goal OSS (Elementary)

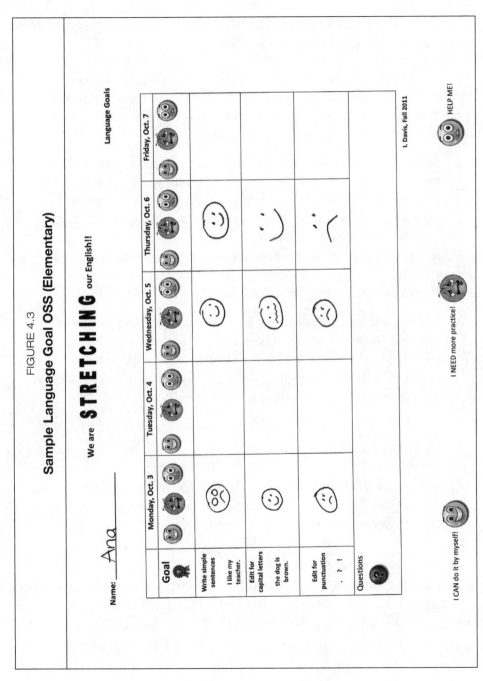

Courtesy of Ileana Davis

Ileana Davis has firsthand evidence of how the use of objective score sheets can change students' learning habits:

> No longer do my students think they are just generally learning English; with an OSS, they know the specific skills they are working on each week. With the use of simple smiley faces, they can tell me how they feel about each skill we are working on in each lesson.
>
> At first, most of my students were putting all happy faces or all sad faces on their goal sheet, thinking that was what I wanted to see. But as we have used the objective score sheets more, I am seeing the students become more honest about whether or not they understand. A very quiet little girl in the group has now approached me and said, "Mrs. Davis, I don't know how to write a sentence." For her to come to me and be able to articulate what she didn't understand and what she needed help with is a huge testament the value of using an OSS for language standards.
>
> I didn't know how powerful a simple form for understanding English language learning standards could be—both for the students and for me. As teachers, if we never ask our students to think about their own learning or reflect on their own progress, they are always going to be dependent on someone else to tell them how they are doing.

✂ Time to Reflect ✂

How might you design objective score sheets to help students self-assess, communicate with you about their progress, and take a more active role in their language learning?

Some teachers raise the question of whether setting and pursuing separate language goals with ELLs in an inclusion classroom might lead to embarrassment and resistance. This is a valid concern, but it is also an outcome that can largely be avoided through discretion. Teacher Karen DuChene says, "With all the language levels in my co-taught math class, I discreetly individualize the language goal by giving students note cards with the appropriate daily goal.

I teach and give feedback during the lesson, and at the end of the lesson, the students have the opportunity to self-assess. The note cards are laminated, so we can reuse them as needed."

Jill Jones, a 4th grade teacher, adds, "My students keep a notebook of their language goals, so we choose and score goals to work on during the lesson. It is a personal and diplomatic approach for my middle school students, who may not want specific attention drawn to their language learning."

Although we believe it is right to approach this sensitive issue with caution, we are ultimately encouraged by teachers' reports of the pride students feel when they make clear gains in their language learning. The objective score sheets mark and communicate this advancement; for the majority of students, they are evidence that the effort they invest yields real dividends.

Tracking Performance on Language Goals

As a complement to providing clear language goals expressed in ELL-friendly terms at the beginning of each lesson, a teacher can also use a language goal tracking form based on grade level and students' language proficiency level to monitor every student's progress toward those language goals. Think of it as a way to link the goal setting at the beginning of the lesson (the first "G" of GANAG) to the goal review at the end of the lesson (the second "G"). Figure 4.4 on page 100 shows a partially completed example of this type of goal tracking form, designed for 1st graders' first unit of the school year.

Throughout instruction, the teacher can keep track of student performance data derived from assignments or obtained through observation. The live, or "prime time," scoring that the teacher or EL specialist does during instruction can be shared with students as formative feedback as long as doing so does not interrupt their learning. Over the course of several lessons, the data collected can reveal illuminating patterns and can be helpful for planning and differentiating future instruction.

EL specialists and other teachers working with ELLs can keep these separate running records of language goals (related to reading, writing, speaking, and listening) much like an elementary teacher keeps track of student

FIGURE 4.4
Sample Goal Tracking Sheet

CC Focus Standard(s)	Demonstrate command of the conventions of standard English grammar and usage when writing and speaking.										
Strand	**ELPW.7.K-2.14**				**ELPW.9.K-2.1**				**ELPW.9.K-2.2**		
English Language Proficiency Standard To Be Measured	Edit simple sentences with teacher support and full class participation: capitalization, begin/end punctuation, develop personal vocab dictionary, give and receive feedback.				Write simple sentences around known words, repetitive phrases, and sentence beginnings to incorporate transition words and combine sentences correctly.				Use the syntax or oral language: singular and plural pronouns, subject and verb agreement in simple sentences.		
Student/Dates	9-28 PARTNER	9-29 CONVO	10-3 STORE	10-12 S.W.	9-28 CREATE	9-29 CONVO	10-3 STORE	10-12 S.W.	10-3 STORE	10-12 STORE	10-14 DESCR.PTR
Arturo	2	1	3	1 (PUNC)	2	2	3	2	2	2	3
Sara	1	1	1 (CAP)	2	2	2	2	2	1	2	–
Ana	1	1	1	1	3	3	2	1	1	1	–
Alex	2	1	3		3	2	2		2		
Asiram	2		2	2 (CAP)	2		2	2	2		
Nameni	1	2	1	1 (PUNC)	1	2	1	2	1	2	
David	2	2	3	2	2	2	3	2	2	3	
Dani	1	1	1	2	3	2	1	2	1	2	–

Student/Dates	10-14 DESCR.PTR				10-14 CESCR.PTR						
Arturo	3				3						
Sara	–				–						
Ana	2				2						
Alex	1 (CAPS)				3						
Asiram	–				–						
Nameni	2				2						
David	2				2						
Dani	(1-1)				(1-1)						

Courtesy of Ileana Davis

performances in the various subject areas taught in a K–5 classroom. It is an approach that allows for clearer monitoring of gains and setbacks in proficiency over the course of daily and weekly lessons, and thus more immediate responses and adjustments. Critically, it eliminates the need to wait for the results of level testing, which usually does not take place until the third quarter of the school year.

At first glance, this goal-setting and tracking process may seem like "a lot of work" or "too much grading," but any teacher who has also coached—either sports or the performing arts—knows the value of tracking or scoring performances as a way to encourage intrinsic motivation and to show the learner how to improve. Yes, teachers and students are busy and have multiple responsibilities, but using language goal self-assessment forms and tracking sheets is a truly effective way to ensure that teachers are being more deliberate in teaching English language and providing more targeted feedback to help students develop English proficiency. Criterion-based feedback is key to reducing the gap between the learner's current level of English language knowledge and skill and the goals for language proficiency.

Here are some of Ileana's comments about using tracking sheets:

> When I started using the tracking sheets, I noticed that I became much more aware of students making progress from week to week. This led me to deliberately assign language tasks to students in areas where they needed help with language acquisition rather than simply giving them compliments or credit for what they were already doing well. It made me much more purposeful with my instruction, since I knew what they knew. The students sensed they really were getting better and learning more, and this seemed to motivate them to do even more.

Once the practice of tracking daily student performance relative to language goals is established, teachers are in a much better position to communicate effectively with both students and parents. Teachers who begin to track student proficiency on language goals *with the students* often find those students more motivated to talk about their progress and more open to communicating in general about their positive school experiences. Danling Fu (2004) writes,

"We need to remember that ELL students know more than what their English language ability enables them to express. Helping ELL students develop their oral language ability is crucial in the overall literacy development. They cannot master the language unless they speak the language" (p. 10).

Harper and de Jong (2004) put it this way:

> Exposure and interactions are simply not enough. ELLs need explicit opportunities to practice using the new language to negotiate meaning in interactive settings. Teachers need to draw students' attention to the structure of the English language used in specific academic context and provide appropriate feedback that ELLs can use to further their oral and written academic language development. (p. 154)

By focusing on a good set of articulated language learning goals, teachers are moving toward minding the gap by creating a manageable, motivating, and deliberate academic and language environment in every classroom. Gersten and Baker (2000) state that teachers often lack an effective means of providing feedback to ELLs in a manner that allows for timely correction of errors. It is this formative feedback that prompts students to self-correct English usage before allowing themselves to accept their errors as correct.

✖ Time to Reflect ✖

How might you or the teachers in your school begin tracking student progress toward language goals? What are the first steps?

In this section we emphasized the benefits of using language learning goals on a daily or lesson-by-lesson basis, but this certainly does not replace other forms of assessment for language and content. Traditional forms of assessment (e.g., paper/pencil tests or quizzes, timed responses on assessment measures) will continue to be used, with appropriate teacher modifications to allow ELLs the opportunity to demonstrate their knowledge. This may mean creating oral tests as opposed to written ones and perhaps implementing prompts to cue students as to the content being tested.

Even though EL teachers and classroom teachers can help ELLs focus on language learning skills, they must also address subject-area content goals for these students to help them stay abreast of their peers in content knowledge, a goal that is unquestionably easier to reach as students become more proficient in the English language. Ileana captured this accurately when she stated, "Minding the achievement gap for ELLs requires teachers and specialists to look to GANAG to deliberately teach content *and* English language standards."

GANAG as the Framework for Pursuing Content and Language Goals

With the two "G"s of GANAG established and deliberately connected to the English language standards frameworks as well as to the Common Core State Standards, Ileana and her EL specialist colleagues started to use GANAG for lesson planning and delivery. They saw it as a way to emphasize goal pursuit and maximize feedback to students and as a way to more effectively coordinate their English language instruction with classroom teachers' content instruction. (See Chapter 5 for a more detailed discussion of using GANAG with co-teaching.) Figure 4.5 on page 104 shows a map of an EL specialist's workweek, noting the content and language goals for each group of students the specialist will be working with and the GANAG structure of each lesson.

The process of lesson coordination is straightforward. Working alone or with an EL specialist, the teacher specifies one or more language goals (state-written, WIDA, or from another language source) that might focus on reading (R), writing (W), listening (L), or speaking (S) and correspond with or otherwise support attainment of the lesson's content goals. Then the classroom teacher or EL specialist sets an expectation for each student's achievement based on tested proficiency and the benchmarks provided by the selected standards.

Figure 4.6 on page 105 shows an example of using GANAG to deliberately address the language goals within the context of a general education

FIGURE 4.5

An EL Specialist's GANAGed Workweek

Ileana Davis — ESOL Teacher   Week of: 10/17–10/21

Class Session	Content Objective	Language Objective	Monday	Tuesday	Wednesday	Thursday	Friday
7:45–8:05 1st grade ELL 2	- Use singular and plural pronouns in simple sentences.	- Describe pictures using pronouns.	Professional Development	3rd – 5th grade DATA DAY	G goal sheet A sing. pronouns/pix N partners G goal sheet	G goal sheet A sing. pnouns/T-chart N plural pronouns A T-chart/S.W. G goal sheet	SmartBoard games: pronouns 1-on-1 conferences
8:05–8:30 1st grade ELL 1	- Write simple sentences around known words.	- Use cloze sentences with picture cards to create simple sentences.			G objective A who/what + action A buddy writing G objective	G objective A parts of a sentence N rotation writing A individual writing w/clozes	iPods: iSentence SmartBoard: "Name that sound"
9:00–9:30 1st grade ELL 1 & 2	- Summarize content of nonfiction using a variety of strategies.	- Read passage for content. - Use web to organize info. - Write a response.	G objective A bears? N fluency passage A read; important facts		G objective A starfish/ocean N fluency passage A buddy read (new info) G objective Starfish	G objective A fluency passage N webs A create/fill webs G objective Starfish	(Friday schedule) Writing conferences – organization – complete sentences – details
9:30–10:00 Kindergarten ELL 1	- Experiment with language.	- Change a letter to create word family. - Begin writing simple sight words.	G objective A letters make words N word/pic change beginning A Big Book G objective		G objective A letters make words N letter cards G objective "What happens when we ...?"	G objective A letters make words N focus sight words A shared writing G objective	iPods: ABC Go SmartBoard: ABC Sort
10:00–11:00 5th grade ELL 1 & 2	- Write a variety of sentences. - Organize writing to develop a draft.	- Use simple and compound sentences to write a description [of candy].	G objective A candy N simple/comp. compare A fluency passage G objective Candy		G objective A candy; simple/comp. N nouns/verbs A passage search G objective Candy	G objective A simple/compound nouns & verbs N "Plan" candy A prewriting G objective	SmartBoard: types of sentences (Koosh Ball game) iPods: Storybuilder
12:05–12:40 2nd grade ELL 2	- Read simple informational books (passages) for specific information.	- Read passage for content. - Use flow chart to organize info. - Write a response.	Finish flow chart from last week.		G objective A parks: what to do? (list) N passage A add new info G objective City Parks	G objective A passage: parks N flow chart A buddy read; pick 3 to do G objective	G objective A flow chart N adding info to chart A write out steps G objective
1:00–1:40 2nd grade ELL 1	- Classify materials as transparent, translucent, or opaque.	- Define key vocab. - ID properties (w/pix). - Classify materials (sorting).	G objective A Columbus N What? What? When? Whose? G objective Finish; on to science		G objective A Brain Pop - light N key vocabulary A picture representation G objective	G objective A light N properties (++) A experiment G objective SmartBoard lesson	G objective A experiment N write statements A object sort G objective

Weekly Objectives

Courtesy of Ileana Davis

FIGURE 4.6

GANAG and Sample Content and Language Goals for a Science Lesson

Lesson Phases	Content Goal (CG) and Procedures	Language Goal (LG) and Procedures
G	Science Content Goal: *Know how to use the pH scale to characterize acid and base solutions.* Students write goal in their science notebooks and score themselves.	**LG, Writing, Level 2:** *Make comparisons [classify] using real-life materials.* **LG, Speaking, Level 3:** *Answer simple, content-based questions.* ELLs write CG in notebooks; use separate, objective score sheets for LGs. Teacher will provide feedback to ELLs specific to LGs, but also regarding language control.
A	Teacher shows iTunes icon screenshot and asks students to write three reasons why they like to use it to classify their music and movies. Briefly, items classified make usage more efficient. Make analogy to liquids and food chart and their pH levels.	ELLs answer simple content-based questions regarding iTunes and the analogy; the teacher can cue or use short but clearly articulated sentence starters to encourage language use.
N	Mini-lecture: pH, what it is, the scale, and the importance of understanding pH, such as dangers. Students take notes. Students pair-share a few times to clear misconceptions about content. Students draw and label pH scale.	ELLs write vocabulary in prepared notes or advance organizer about pH. Teacher restates or models correct language usage, providing synonyms or simplified explanations. ELLs work cooperatively with other students.
A	Given 12 liquids, students • Test and discuss (in lab group of four students) • Record results • Draw conclusions To share findings with class use the "CO_2" summarizing strategy of giving a conclusion based on two observations: C – Conclusion and O_2 – 2 Observations	Teacher and students give corrective feedback on accurate vocabulary and confirm conceptual understanding. Students generate questions and hypotheses by answering simple content-based questions.
G	Students write two or more sentences in their notebooks, using the prompt, "I used to think, but now I know . . ." Students rescore themselves on the original learning goal for the lesson.	ELLs write and speak to prompt, with the teacher supporting with vocabulary and sentence structure feedback. Teacher and ELLs score progress on same criteria, the CG and LGs.

Source for Language Goals: English Language Development Standards, State of Colorado science lesson (here, one about using the pH scale to indicate the acidity and alkalinity levels). Throughout the lesson, as an ELL performs and is prompted by the teacher or an interventionist, he or she may receive corrective feedback on the targeted language goal, which can be unpacked to more specifically address language use and which functions within the context of a content goal.

As this lesson progresses, a teacher can use a goal-specific tracking sheet and a grading scale (e.g., 4-3-2-1) to score all students, including ELLs, on content goals by walking around during the "liquid testing lesson," looking at the student notes, listening to students while they test the liquids, and asking questions. "Half" scores may be used to provide more discriminating feedback to students. An EL specialist, if present, might use a separate tracking sheet and similar assessment scale to score ELLs on their progress toward the lesson's language goals. A classroom teacher might take on this task as well, assisted by a form modified to show the specific writing and speaking goals addressed in the science lesson and with additional space to note indicators of individual student progress toward those goals.

Within the GANAG framework, these assessment procedures allow teachers to make formative adjustments to the ways in which they will present the lesson's new information (the "N" of GANAG) or the lesson's application and practice activities (the second "A" of GANAG). Further student-generated feedback and reflection on these lesson stages, as well as on the generalization and self-assessment that wraps up a lesson, can be captured in an interactive notebook (see Chapter 3) and used formatively to inform the next stages of planning—the new goals that students will pursue and the most effective ways to achieve these goals.

Time to Reflect

Think of a specific lesson you teach and consider how teaching, tracking, and providing daily feedback on language and content goals and in a GANAG structure would change the way you deliver this lesson.

As is the case with any lessons planned and delivered in the GANAG format, lessons with integrated content and language goals include student learning strategies such as working cooperatively, generating questions and hypotheses, and using advance organizers. The incorporation of high-yield strategies, modified for ELLs, helps students progress more rapidly toward achieving language and content goals. Modifying the strategies supports a teacher's efforts to mind the achievement gap.

Modifying the Nine High-Yield Strategies for ELLs

The use of language goals is a big part of minding the gap for ELLs, but we also recommend emphasizing the nine high-yield strategies within the GANAG framework of a lesson. When we make this recommendation, teachers typically ask us two questions: (1) "Am I supposed to be using the high-yield strategies with ELLs?" and (2) "Am I supposed to modify the strategies for ELLs?"

Jane Hill and Kathleen M. Flynn (2006) wrote that there is an "urgent need to improve the quantity and quality of instruction for ELLs both in special programs and in basic classrooms" (p. viii). Using the research from *Classroom Instruction That Works* (Marzano et al., 2001), Hill and Flynn examined and modified the nine strategies for use with ELLs. We suggest that teachers start with their book, *Classroom Instruction That Works with English Language Learners* (2006), to make developmentally appropriate use of the strategies.

When a teacher uses the GANAG schema to plan lessons that will maximize both high-yield instructional strategies and opportunities for ongoing feedback, adaptations for ELLs should be deliberate and explicit. It is a matter of aligning procedures that are generally recommended as modifications for ELLs to the high-yield strategies.

For example, teachers can provide scaffolds in the form of prepared or partially prepared notes that model and build vocabulary (summarize and take notes, $d = 1.00$). They can maximize opportunities for ELLs to use drawings or other visuals, physical body movement, and objects (nonlinguistic representations, $d = 0.75$). The strategies are ones that all students in the class can use, and we encourage teachers to modify their instruction to maximize the likelihood that ELLs will learn to use these strategies well.

⚔ Time to Reflect ⚔

In what ways could you modify the nine high-yield strategies to effectively adapt them in support of the individual language abilities of your students?

GANAG and SIOP

Some teachers note that it is possible to blend GANAG with the popular Sheltered Instruction Observation Protocol (SIOP), championed by Echevarria, Vogt, and Short (2004). It makes sense, as SIOP involves observing teachers to monitor their use of teaching strategies (e.g., visuals; short, simple sentences; clear and expressive articulation; and high-frequency vocabulary) intended to help ELLs be successful in both inclusion and resource classrooms. Since GANAG is a lesson delivery model that guides students to intentionally use high-yield strategies, and SIOP is a classroom observation protocol, the tools can work in a complementary fashion to improve instructional efficiency and increase student learning.

Many teachers find that aligning the 30 features of SIOP with GANAG makes them more manageable for both planning and delivery (see Figure 4.7).

⚔ Time to Reflect ⚔

What contributions might blending GANAG and SIOP make to teaching ELLs in your school and district?

Schedules and the Standards-Based Curriculum

A teacher from Wisconsin wrote to us looking for guidance:

FIGURE 4.7 The GANAG Schema Aligned with SIOP	
GANAG	**SIOP**
G: Set clear standards and objectives.	**Preparation:** – Provide clear content objectives/language objectives.
A: Guide students to access prior knowledge and experience.	**Building Background:** – Link concepts to students' background experiences. – Link past concepts and new concepts.
N: Use a variety of effective instructional strategies to bring new information, knowledge, and skills to students.	**Preparation:** – Use meaningful, integrated learning activities. **Comprehensible Input:** – Use speech appropriate to students' language proficiency. – Provide clear explanation for academic tasks. **Strategies:** – Use scaffolding techniques. – Use tasks that promote the use of thinking skills. **Lesson Delivery:** – Support content objectives and language objectives. – Aim for high student engagement (90–100%). – Ensure appropriate lesson pacing. **Interaction:** – Use sufficient teacher wait time. – Provide ample opportunities for the clarification of key concepts. – Use grouping configurations. – Use interactive processes.
A: Provide opportunities for students to use thinking skills to apply new knowledge to real-world situations.	**Practice/Application:** – Use hands-on materials and manipulatives. – Provide opportunities for students to apply content and language knowledge in the classroom. – Choose activities that integrate all language skills.
G: Have students generalize and review their progress toward goals.	**Review/Assessment:** – Review key vocabulary. – Review key concepts.
HOMEWORK: Extend the school day with practice and application activities.	**Practice/Application:** – Integrate all language skills.
ASSESSMENT and FEEDBACK: Implement formative assessment throughout the lesson, providing specific and timely feedback to students to further guide/support their learning.	**Review/Assessment:** – Gather formative assessment data on student comprehension and learning throughout the instructional process. – Provide students with regular, specific, and timely feedback based on formative assessment.

Adapted with permission from Jessica Sallis, ESOL specialist, Rogers Public Schools

We have 25 English language learners coming to our school next year. I, personally, have no experience or training in this area, and I am concerned about meeting the needs of the new students. We are told that the students' levels of fluency range from little or no English to quite fluent. I am not certain how to prepare or implement lessons that will enable these children to learn, and I think this is the case for most teachers in our building.

It does not appear that the district can provide professional development for us at this time, but we do have a part-time EL specialist who will service the 25 students; I simply cannot imagine how one part-time teacher can possibly meet with multiple teachers. And what do we do for a curriculum? Does it need to be standards-based?

In two paragraphs, this teacher captures the key parts of the conundrum: the schedule and the standards-based curriculum. Due to the unpredictable number of ELLs in school and their varying levels of language proficiency, scheduling is complicated. Sometimes students with vastly different levels of language proficiency are grouped together in a single setting, leaving teachers unsure of how to approach the planning and delivery of lessons. Depending on the service delivery model, the teacher's role varies from being a consulting teacher or a co-teacher in a classroom to assisting in support classes, such as pull-out and resource-model classes. The wide range of student proficiency and teacher expectations can create havoc in scheduling and weaken the continuity of working toward sequenced standards.

Classroom teachers like the letter writer from Wisconsin benefit from knowing that using GANAG provides a structured lesson that is equally appropriate for general education students and English language learners. EL teachers should deliberately use success criteria to set the standards-based learning intentions (for language separate from but linked to content), teach to the learning intentions, and improve and expand their use of feedback to include student self-assessment. Any teacher, interventionist or classroom teacher, can learn to adapt lessons with high-yield strategies to make them more effective for ELLs, making modifications that allow for full participation and focused pursuit of the content standards. Planning and teaching in this manner allows ELLs to participate fully in lessons designed to content standards, thus easing some scheduling concerns.

Taking New, Deliberately Coordinated Action

Many of the recent reforms aimed at increasing the academic achievement of ELLs have focused on the placement and testing of students and the scheduling of teaching and support services. While these reforms are necessary, they address school structure rather than aspects of daily instructional practices in inclusion classrooms, which is where the most significant difference can be made. However, shifting focus to pedagogical practices requires even experienced educators to adjust their teaching. To us, the answer lies in making the language and content goals and success criteria clear to English language learners, planning for and instructing these students to use high-yield strategies, and providing them with effective and frequent feedback.

Educator Voice
Julie Housaman, District Administrator

Julie Housaman, a Title III coordinator, is convinced of the benefits of having ELL students included in general education classrooms. The key, Julie
explains, is for teachers, both general education and EL specialists, to have
a learning plan and strategies for a new, more successful kind of inclusion.

Success for Every English Language Learner

Over the years, the population of English language learners in our district has
increased, and to accommodate these students, we opened and provided trans-
portation to "Center Schools"—two at the elementary level, one at the middle
school level, and one at the high school level—that featured self-contained
classrooms in which certified bilingual or English as a Second Language (ESL)
teachers taught ELLs.

When the buzz began throughout the district that new policy would integrate Center School students who had been learning in self-contained classrooms into the general education classrooms of their neighborhood schools,
the ensuing conversations I had with teachers and administrators were marked
by a mixture of excitement and apprehension. Language teachers from Center
Schools were concerned that they would be put to use as educational assistants;
classroom teachers were anxious about how to meet the needs of students
with varying levels of English proficiency. School principals praised the clearly

defined process for scheduling students in classrooms and requested ongoing professional development to build a common knowledge base among staff.

We knew that professional development for both teachers and administrators was essential to meeting our goal: ensuring that all children, especially our ELLs, would be successful in our new inclusion classrooms. Both classroom teachers and language teachers needed support to improve the quality of their instructional practices. Administrators also needed assistance to better understand how students acquire language and what their expectations should be for language and classroom teachers. Peggy Black met with our staff and provided direction in how to establish language goals within content lessons. She also showed us how GANAG could provide a solid foundation for meeting the needs of ELLs in general education classrooms.

Goal Setting

Questions still loomed large as we began to prepare for this change. How would language teachers support ELLs with varying language levels and at different grade levels? How should we define the roles of general education teachers and EL teachers?

We began by designing a job description for the language teachers that included collaboration, consultation, and co-teaching methods as the means to build effective working relationships with classroom teachers. Professional development focused on goal setting and began with a review of the research. An audience of more than 40 language teachers eagerly listened and nodded in agreement with the concept; however, questions and concerns regarding the "how to" were prevalent.

How It Worked

Sensing the anxiety of our staff, I encouraged frequent communication with me as the school year began. A few teachers and their stories stood out.

Nathan is an elementary school language teacher who was apprehensive about working with classroom teachers. He discovered that he was integrated into the general classroom from day one and went in armed with the WIDA Can-Do descriptors as language goals. He said, "I wasn't just helping, I was teaching cooperatively with the classroom teacher. It was so enjoyable!"

On the first day of school, Jillian, a middle school language teacher, encountered a veteran history teacher in the hall who had several ELLs in his class. During the past three years, those students had been pulled out of the classroom for history instruction with Jillian. The history teacher was anxious to schedule Jillian to work with the language students outside his classroom on a regular basis. Jillian began her response to him by focusing on the positive strategies that he currently used to support language learners, and she went on to explain the benefit of in-class support for both these students and himself. Although the teacher's reluctance was evident, he did schedule a meeting with Jillian to review the students' individual language plans (ILPs). He also agreed to have Jillian model how language instruction could be integrated into content lessons in such a way that it monitored student progress toward both the history content goals and English language goals. Afterward, the veteran classroom teacher had this to say: "I see how this can work, and I would like you to provide support in the classroom."

Administrators supported this new method of teaching by ensuring that ELLs were clustered based on language levels in general education classrooms, grouping predominantly beginning speakers in one classroom, intermediate speakers in another, and so on. Language teachers, now in inclusion classrooms, worked to ensure that language goals and content goals were addressed. They were able to correct and support students' language learning accuracy to help keep them on track with their goals. Classroom teachers could see content goals as being an intrinsic part of lessons, and making the connection between content and language goals became natural for many teachers.

Specific goals have helped students pay attention to what they need to focus on in each lesson. Language teachers are assisting classroom teachers in developing these goals by asking, "How do you want students to be able to communicate to you what they know?" General education teachers who questioned how they would meet the needs of ELLs in their classrooms were given an encouragingly simple answer: by addressing language goals within the content lessons.

The Future Is Bright

This is an exciting journey for students, teachers, parents, and administrators. As one language teacher shared, "These changes were needed, and they are working!" I concur with this statement. As the coordinator of Title III programs for our district, I recently reviewed standardized test data comparing the performance of English language learners in Center Schools to that of students in general education classrooms in neighborhood schools. I saw that ELLs in general education classrooms performed as well as, and in many cases better than, their cohorts who had been in the Center Schools' self-contained classrooms.

We continue to face challenges as we move forward, but with the focus on each child becoming proficient in both content and English language development, I am confident we will continue to see academic growth. The work is significant in addressing how all teachers will successfully meet the learning needs of language students *today*, because tomorrow is not soon enough for our students.

5

Increasing Achievement in Special Education

ALTHOUGH THE ACHIEVEMENT GAPS THAT TEND TO RECEIVE THE most attention from the media and politicians are those related to race and class, there's another, less discussed gap that is nevertheless of great concern to both educators and parents: the low academic performance of many students receiving special education services. *Washington Post* education columnist Jay Mathews (2009) captures the complicated nature of this topic very well:

> I admit that education writers in general, and I in particular, write very little about learning disabilities and the many failures of federally mandated public school programs to help students who have them. I often say the cases are so complicated I have difficulty translating them into everyday language, and even then readers struggle to understand. But that is not the whole truth.

> I also avoid special education stories because they all seem the same, one tale after another of frustrated parents and ill-equipped educators trying but failing to find common ground, calling in lawyers while the children sit in class, bored and confused. That is not a good reason for ignoring what is probably the most aggravating part of our public school system, at least for the millions of parents who have to deal with it.

The education of children in special education programs may be less prominent in the general conversation about achievement gaps, but in our experience it is a *high priority* for teachers and administrators. It is without question a priority under No Child Left Behind legislation. In both self-contained resource and inclusion classrooms, special educators work diligently to create a positive environment and prepare challenging lessons for students receiving special education services. Today, students classified as having learning disabilities or needing special education are likely to be learning in an environment that is more positive and less restrictive than special education has ever been. They are likely to have access not only to a curriculum that is more challenging but also to individualized support services aimed at helping them achieve their goals. Unfortunately, these structural improvements to the process of special education have not necessarily resulted in higher achievement for special education students.

Consistent with the theme of this book, we believe that the key to increasing achievement for any students, special education students included, is to shift the reform attention from school structures and toward what a teacher (or collaborating teachers) can do with the help of research-based instructional practices within an individual classroom.

Co-Teaching in Inclusion Classrooms: A Structural Effort to Close the Gap

As more and more schools adjust classroom organization, schedules, and service delivery models to better accommodate the needs of various kinds of learners, the traditional model of "one teacher, one classroom" is changing. In the wake of the 2004 reauthorized Individuals with Disabilities Education Improvement Act, more and more students classified as having disabilities and special needs are being educated through "inclusion," in regular classroom settings alongside typically achieving peers. This shift has given rise to co-teaching, an arrangement in which professional educators (usually a general classroom teacher and a teacher who specializes in learning disabilities) share a single physical space and instructional responsibilities, working together to design and deliver lessons and support the academic growth of every student in the classroom.

While it seems logical that "two heads are better than one"—and that two professionals working together with a classroom of students will increase the likelihood of success—many who co-teach note that co-teaching has not, in fact, had much effect on special education students' test scores, either on common assessments or state tests. This is a perception mirrored by research findings. Marilyn Friend and DeAnna Hurley-Chamberlain, proponents of co-teaching models, write on the website of the Council for Exceptional Children (www.cec.sped.org) that although there are plenty of studies on the implementation of co-teaching, only recently have studies begun to look at evidence of co-teaching's effectiveness when it comes to improving achievement among students with special needs. Citing various researchers who studied co-/team teaching approaches with special education teachers, John Hattie (2009) reports that the average effect size reported for co-/team teaching is considered low at $d = 0.19$, far short of the $d = 4.0$ bar that signifies an effective instructional practice. He concludes that despite the creativity, enthusiasm, and strength of the teachers who co-teach, the approach currently does not translate into noteworthy student achievement gains.

In addition, many veteran teachers and specialists, although they support the goals of inclusion, admit to approaching co-teaching with trepidation. It is a model of teaching that requires not only new skills but also a new way of working. For example, when Judy Pottle returned to teaching kindergarten after a hiatus of several years, she had some surprises waiting for her. "I'm glad to be back in a classroom," she mused, "but the biggest change since I last taught is that there are five certified adults who work in my room! At first, I have to admit that I wondered, 'What am I supposed to do with them?'" Judy, like many other classroom teachers, was unsure of how to best involve the special education teachers and the paraprofessionals in her room. "How do I co-teach?" she asked.

This question captures the most obvious challenge of a co-teaching arrangement. How does a teacher who learned to work well independently maximize productivity when assigned to work with other educators in *his or her* classroom? Concerns such as those raised by Judy leave professionals feeling anxious about the co-teaching situation rather than confident that the structure of the classroom will make a positive difference for gap students.

Specialist teachers are equally challenged and similarly confused. Many report that their initial view of what co-teaching would be like turned out to be very different from reality. They had imagined planning lessons together, team teaching, and analyzing student work together; instead, they found themselves directed to sit off to the side with "their students." Pat Hamilton, a classroom-based special education teacher in Ohio, described feeling "second-tier"—a perception reinforced when one of her 8th graders sent her a Christmas card addressed "To My Almost-Teacher." (The general education teacher's card was addressed "To My Teacher.")

Lisa Setsor, a district-level special education director, identified three challenges teachers typically face when co-teaching is first implemented:

1. Most teachers, both special education and regular education, have had little or no training in effective co-teaching methods.

2. Some classroom teachers are reluctant to try new methods or give up "control" for the purpose of serving the handful of special education students in the classroom.

3. Almost all teachers worry that they need extensive time to collaborate on planning good lessons and assessments.

The uneasiness surrounding co-teaching might be compared to what a runner familiar with 5Ks and 10Ks would feel when participating in a three-legged race. It is still running, but running while physically bound to another person requires a different skill set. Co-teaching is teaching in collaboration with another professional, so it requires a different approach to planning and delivering instruction.

On top of these challenges, co-teachers must handle the additional complications inherent in teaching students with learning disabilities, many of whom, according to Lisa Setsor, tend to display the following characteristics:

• They lack basic organizational skills and so often do not have materials they need when lesson begins.

• They lack strong note-taking skills or adequate strategies for processing information quickly and efficiently.

• They have low-level reading skills.

• They have trouble retaining material even after they have read it or heard it.

• They demonstrate behaviors that often interfere with learning (sometimes the behaviors are deliberate, undertaken to avoid lessons they view as difficult).

• They feel defeated from years of struggling in school and are often disengaged; they rarely raise their hands, volunteer answers, or ask questions, and they have learned through experience that if they wait, someone will usually tell them the answer.

Reviewing this list, some of the reasons that the *structural solution* of co-teaching has done little to improve the performance of special education students come into focus. Simply adding a second teacher to an inclusion classroom—even when that second teacher is a trained specialist, and even when both co-teachers have the best intentions and individualized education plans (IEPs) for guidance—does not guarantee that special education students will get what they really need to learn. By this, we mean deliberate instruction in organizational skills and note taking, ways to overcome reading and retention challenges, and techniques to overcome the sense of defeat that leads to disengagement and the negative behavior. But these students also need what every student needs: lessons that begin with a clear goal and offer opportunity to access prior knowledge, acquire and practice new information and skills, and learn and use high-yield strategies to seek and apply feedback that will help them master the goal.

✳ Time to Reflect ✾

How do teachers in your school approach and manage co-teaching?

Once more we must ask what solution to the problem might be invisible in plain sight? While co-teaching certainly represents a structural change from the "resource room approach," the somersault question to ask is whether the pedagogical innovation co-teaching makes available is being utilized in the best way. Consider how various professionals from different fields (city manager, construction superintendent, geologist) might get together for the purpose of building a bridge. All may come in determined to do good work, but if they lack the right tool to support effective collaboration—perhaps a topographic map—their discussions will flounder. Even if they are able to get the project under way, and even if each professional works as hard as he or she can, absent the critical guidance of the topographical map, the outcome will be a very unsound bridge.

Simply put, the key to better learning outcomes in any classroom is more effective instruction. In a co-taught classroom, where two professionals work in concert to meet the needs of a diverse body of students who may be pursuing very different goals, the key is more effective *coordination* or synchronization of more effective instruction. Teachers can coordinate their plan books and grade books with the curriculum. They can adapt GANAG to improve student learning.

Co-Teaching with GANAGPlus:
A Synchronized Approach to Minding the Gap

When it comes to co-teaching, the chief questions in teachers' minds generally relate to preparation, responsibility, and outcomes. The most common questions are "Who should take the lead during instructional time?" and "How can we assess achievement progress in a classroom with such diversity?" Educators can find answers to both these questions and the map for more effective co-teaching in an expanded form of GANAG, dubbed GANAGPlus. It provides new clarity on roles and responsibilities and a shared approach to instructional planning, delivery, and assessment. It is worth noting that although the discussion in this chapter focuses on improving the learning of students who receive special education services, the alignment of models for co-teaching and the GANAGPlus adaption are transferrable to any classroom where educators work together to enhance the learning of all students.

Synchronized Instruction

The GANAGPlus schema helps co-teachers connect the sequence of effective instruction with strategically selected co-teaching models in order to synchronize both teaching and assessment. To clarify, we will look first at the various models of co-teaching and then at a classroom example that illustrates the achievement-boosting power of GANAGPlus within a co-teaching environment.

Models of co-teaching. The essential idea of co-teaching is that professionals assigned to a classroom share a single physical space and the work of daily lesson delivery in order to better serve a diverse population of students, including those with who might once have been educated in separate special education classrooms.

There are many ways to organize co-teaching responsibilities. Typical models include the following:

• *Parallel teaching:* The class is split into two equal-sized groups, each having the same lesson taught at the same time. Co-teachers work with smaller groups, thus allowing them to better assess students' understanding of content that is being presented. This is often a good model to use when introducing new lesson goals and content, because students are more likely to seek and receive feedback in a smaller group.

• *Small group/large group (split teaching):* Students requiring additional support are placed in a small group, with each group simultaneously receiving the same instruction. When this choice of model is used in class, teachers can pace discussion differently for special populations of students. Student groupings are determined by student learning needs, and this places students in groups where they feel more free to express their questions about content. This model can work well when applying and generalizing about what has been learned in a lesson and discussing further steps with students to reinforce learning.

• *Station teaching:* Small student groups are created for practice or content focus. Teachers rotate to work with different students. In inclusion classrooms, small groups can be created that allow for interaction between general and special education students. As students work together in these groups, they can give each other feedback to support each other's learning. This model often works well when students are practicing and applying content material that has been taught previously.

• *Team teaching:* Teachers use a tag-team delivery in which they appear to extemporaneously step forward or retreat from the main teaching role as needed. Each teacher in a co-taught classroom has knowledge and skills to bring to every lesson. By taking turns stepping forward to share content or to elicit questions from students, they can share this expertise and provide different teaching styles to learners. The students benefit by experiencing content through different frames of expertise and, especially, by hearing new information explained and even repeated in different ways, which helps them make connections and retain the knowledge.

• *One teach, one assist:* A lead teacher delivers the lesson, and the other teacher assists by providing feedback and reteaching. While one teacher instructs, the other moves among students to track learning progress toward specific learning targets. This is a model that works particularly well when new information is being presented to the entire class. The teacher who moves among students gathers data that can be used to identify students to work together at differentiated learning stations or in small groups.

• *One teach, one observe:* The teacher who is assisting carefully observes student performances while the lead teacher delivers a lesson. These observations inform both teachers' subsequent adjustments to instruction and assessment. This model is often a good one to use when prior knowledge is being accessed in the lesson, as the teacher observing students can look for verbal as well as nonverbal clues about background knowledge that may be helpful in understanding current student attitudes and enthusiasm toward the lesson content.

Figure 5.1 on page 124 offers a sample map of which of the co-teaching models might be used within the steps of a GANAG lesson. As noted, we've dubbed the tool for co-teaching planning and instruction "GANAGPlus," as it prompts co-teachers to work through the established GANAG schema on three levels:

FIGURE 5.1

The Stages of GANAG with Sample Co-Teaching Models

	Lesson Stage	Co-Teaching Models
G	Set Goals	Parallel teaching
A	Access Prior Knowledge	One teach, one assist
N	New Information	One teach, one observe (students)
A	Apply	Station teaching
G	Goal Review/Generalize/Self-Assess	Small group, large group

1. Teachers identify goals for the general education and special education students, including addressing IEP goals.

2. Teachers plan so students use high-yield strategies and receive opportunities for feedback.

3. Teachers determine which model or models of co-teaching best fit each phase of the lesson.

In this way, teachers consider when to use different models of co-teaching in order to differentiate the instruction. As they do this, they take into account factors such as the characteristics of the student populations in the inclusion classroom and any adjustments that they need to make throughout a lesson and unit. In other words, timing for implementation of these models is not set in stone, and teachers can be flexible when deciding which co-teaching model works best for specific content, specific classroom situations, and the learning needs of specific students.

GANAGPlus in practice. Middle school co-teachers Missy Daniels and Vicki Haverland use GANAGPlus to instruct and assess students in an inclusion classroom. Figure 5.2 provides a snapshot of how they follow GANAGPlus to synchronize their instruction (in this example, for an English lesson). Note that Missy, the classroom teacher, and Vicki, the specialist, deliberately identify

	FIGURE 5.2	
	A Sample GANAGPlus Lesson Showing Synchronized Co-Teaching	
Lesson Stage	**Co-Teaching Models**	**Actions and Instructional Strategies**
G	One teach/ one assist	Missy, the general education teacher gives the directions to the whole class to write the **standard** on their score sheets in their interactive notebooks; meanwhile, special education teacher, Vicki, unobtrusively addresses **IEP goals** for some of the students and assists with writing the goal in their own words. The goal is "8.5.11 Identify and analyze the persuasive devices used in written and oral communications (e.g., bandwagon, loaded words, testimonial, plain folks, snob appeal)." Missy asks all students to show with a "fist of five" how much **effort** they plan to exert learning that goal. The co-teachers scan the room to detect any confusion or need to reexplain the goal for students. Vicki records some responses on her teacher tracking sheet.
A	Team teach	Missy and Vicki stand in front of the class and **role-play** a persuasive scenario. Missy tries to convince Vicki that she should teach the lesson, but Vicki retreats. While the students watch, Missy uses various persuasive techniques to finally convince Vicki to teach the lesson. Since the teachers are role playing, the students are surprised at first, but watch the persuasion. After a minute or two, the teachers divulge their skit an ask students to **shoulder-partner** to **respond to the cue** to identify two ways that Missy used "persuasion" to convince Vicki to teach. When students respond as a class, Missy and Vicki write some of the responses on the board, indicating specific techniques used in persuasion. Both teachers interact with all of the students.
N	One teach/ one observe students	To teach the content about persuasive devices, the teachers provide the students with a **graphic organizer** to tape into their notebooks to **take notes** about the definitions and devices. One student with an IEP receives an almost completed sheet with blanks to finish. As Missy teaches from the electronic whiteboard, Vicki observes student work to determine whether or not to group students for the application of the content; she uses a clipboard with a seating chart and the objectives as a way to track student performance.
A	Small group/ large group	Missy and Vicki split the class into a large group and a small group. Vicki has the special education students in the small group with a few other students to differentiate the instruction. Missy's **group generates skits in pairs** (the way they saw the teachers role-play) using the **persuasive devices.** Vicki's group reviews the devices and practices predicting which one used when Vicki offers some scenarios. Students from first group perform a skit and the second group **predicts** which one is used and how they perceived the effectiveness of the persuasive device. They wrap up by **summarizing** the importance of **using different persuasive devices** in oral conversation. The next day, they will continue with persuasive devices in written communication so the teachers assign a reading about using persuasion in expository writing and ask students to **take notes** about it in their notebooks.
G	One teach/ one observe	Students take out their objective score sheets to revisit the goal **effort.** Vicki conducts the goal review while Missy walks around scoring students on the clipboard form.

what they will do during each phase of the lesson, which co-teaching model they will use (and who will take which role within that model), and how high-yield strategies (in bold) will be incorporated into the lesson to ensure opportunities for feedback and increased student engagement.

Looking at this example of how these teachers plan and deliver lessons, you may wonder how much time they have to plan together each week. The answer is none—at least, no regular, dedicated, face-to-face time. "We don't have a common planning period," Missy says. They do, however, e-mail their lessons in the GANAGPlus format as a practical way to "discuss" instruction and assessment strategies, as well as co-teaching methods. The result is that the GANAGPlus schema facilitates communication between co-teachers and supports more efficient and purposeful delivery of instruction and formative assessment.

Vicki wrote the following reflection about using GANAGPlus:

Overall, GANAGPlus has given us, the teacher and specialist, a common structure to work with:

G: Everyone is aware of what we will be working on. Students "own" the lesson more when they have the awareness of what is being taught. In fact, every day the class reads the goal together. We are making more of an effort to address why our students are learning this and how the learning affects their lives.

A: Accessing prior knowledge works! It does seem to "fire" their neurons and pique some interest. Sometimes it is still challenging to find out just how to do this but it always leads to better engagement.

N and **A:** Use of research-based strategies have helped increase our students' involvement and engagement. There seems to be more enthusiasm in the class as a whole, and we give much better feedback. We also have become good at guiding students to seek feedback from peers.

G: All of our students now know that they will be held accountable for the lesson. The goal review activity gives us feedback about different levels of student understanding.

This reflection about our co-teaching process doesn't adequately convey the personal enthusiasm I feel for the process. I am appreciative of the understanding we have gained as educators to help us in doing our jobs more effectively.

✄ Time to Reflect ✄

What changes to your lesson planning and delivery could you and your co-teachers make using GANAGPlus?

Even with best intentions, many educators agree that much work is needed in the area of advancing achievement in special education. Consider the level of concern and commitment to all students' needs in the following comments from a district-level special education director, Chris Meyers, whose school board initially questioned the cost and results of co-teaching:

> "How can you justify having two teachers in a classroom for students if you still are not making AYP (Adequate Yearly Progress)?" It's a valid question, asked by the Board of Education, when considering that some classrooms were drawing more than $120,000 of salary from the special education budget. The Board wanted to know why this system continued to be maintained when, over the course of four years, it still had not produced results on standardized testing.

Chris Myers told us co-teaching survived in his district even though the persistent low scores of the special education population prevented schools from making AYP. As he explained, the sensitive nature of past special education practices, belief systems about student learning, and the complications of scheduling teachers and specialists made it difficult to even discuss the district's approach to co-teaching, let alone revamp it. What he sought was a way to improve teaching practices within the structure of co-teaching, and he was inspired by a famous motivational quotation: "If we want what we have never had, we must be willing to do what we have never done before." Determined to increase student achievement within their existing co-teaching program, Chris introduced staff in his district to GANAG and GANAGPlus. The result, he says, was a synergy of changes in teaching practices that have boosted a collective belief that all students can learn better.

Chris characterizes the classroom-based changes as "improved instructional intensity," and he explains that "instructional intensity is the degree of purpose attributed to each instructional strategy used in a classroom. When there is a clearly defined goal for each lesson, use of various instructional strategies, and a central focus on students learning toward the goal, instructional intensity is at its highest. Now take that intensity and double it! With two teachers in an inclusion classroom, the goals, strategies, and learning are focused in the work of two professionals: two teachers using the GANAG schema double the achievement potential."

Within a year of embracing GANAGPlus, Chris's district made AYP, and it has sustained those gains for four years. "Honestly, the journey was arduous, but the payoff in increased student achievement was well worth it," writes Chris, who worked closely with the district's curriculum director, Dana Paykos. "In my opinion, our catalyst for success began with our collaboration to mind the gap, classroom by classroom, for special education students and for all students," he says.

Here is an interesting analogy for co-teaching shared with us by a middle school teacher who has a license to fly private aircraft. He spoke specifically about aviation safety protocol, which is critically important in order to avoid "cockpit complacency" that can lead to danger or disaster. "Pilots and co-pilots," he told us, "verbally review the ordinary functions of fuselage and flight preparations/operations before every flight in a deliberate effort to anticipate any complications. They check each function together in order to assure thoroughness and expected outcomes, for example, safe take-offs and landings."

Just like pilots who must draw up their flight plans, teachers must develop lesson plans. And, just like pilots and co-pilots, teachers and co-teachers can systematically follow a protocol—here, GANAGPlus—to review the lesson to anticipate any complications, making specific initial checks on their "takeoffs" and "landings"—the bookend "G"s of their GANAGPlus lessons. The format outlines the co-teaching approach that is to be used, academic modifications, behavioral modifications, and instructional considerations given to each lesson. With these aspects of teaching and assessment in place, co-teachers avoid "classroom complacency" and position themselves and their students for success.

⚜ Time to Reflect ⚜

How does the aviation analogy help you to think about the protocol that you must follow together in planning and instructing in co-taught classrooms?

Synchronized Assessment

GANAGPlus guided Mat Gover and Sue Furcinito, two co-teachers in New York, to increase achievement for their special education students. They describe how they used the schema to synchronize their assessment, too. In ways similar to the methods of live scoring described by teachers in the previous chapter (using teacher-developed tracking forms), Mat and Sue used GANAGPlus to redefine formative assessment in their shared classroom, because the model created many opportunities for them to "live score" their students.

According to Mat, when you teach using GANAGPlus, you need to learn to use the word "clipboard" as a verb, because once a learning goal is set at the beginning of the class, the teachers take turns walking around the room, tracking student performances from the first "G" of GANAG (goal setting) to the last (goal review and student self-assessment).

Capturing goal-related data. Once Mat and Sue developed a "flow" for lesson delivery using GANAGPlus, Mat sincerely asked himself what he was supposed to be doing while Sue, the special education teacher, was working with a subset of the class and the rest of the students were working on planned assignments. His answer, his natural response, was to walk around the classroom and interact strategically with students as they worked. What GANAGPlus prompted him to do was add the tool he had been missing: something that would help him track student progress toward the goals and capture formative assessment data that could be used to provide specific instructional feedback and inform specific instructional adjustments. Here is how Mat describes his experience:

Get a clipboard. Sue and I define formative assessment as providing frequent feedback to learners that is directly tied to the curriculum targets for the lesson. The strategies are simple—familiar practices such as response boards, thumbs up/thumbs down, and tickets out the door. We walk around the room assessing each student using a predetermined curriculum target and rubric, and we record individual student progress informally on a roster on a clipboard.

As Mat states, using a simple clipboard with a form that shows student names and the objectives for the lesson offers teachers a way to gather helpful assessment data while engaging in the kind of student interactions that they would be engaging in anyway. Since he and Sue were co-teaching, they had time to take turns observing student work, and a consistent method for scoring and documenting performance allowed them to talk about it after class. They admit they were surprised at how their conversations became so much less focused on their students' behavior and so much more on those students' understanding of the content goals and IEP goals. What's more, gauging the learning progress of each student individually and abandoning the practice of asking group questions that resulted in chorus responses allowed for better differentiation. Simply being able to notice when an individual student was having trouble understanding the lesson goals during a class activity improved these co-teachers' ability to provide targeted support, redirection, or adjustments to instruction—usually immediately, during the class session.

Electronic scoring. Once teachers began to track student progress during class, the next step was to transfer those data to a spreadsheet or a grading program that generated threshold reports or standards-based views of assignments. This is what Mat had to say about the benefits of electronic scoring:

I had always been a typical pencil-and-grade-book teacher, recording all my students' grades by hand and then figuring out averages at the end of the term. In all honesty, I thought that moving to electronic scoring would be the most grueling part of record keeping throughout my journey so far—but it wasn't really all that difficult, and it really paid off. The electronic grade book and spreadsheet showed assignments by the curriculum standards and allowed us to clearly plan and differentiate instruction better for special education students and for *all* students. We are able to see any given student's current standing and where that student is making progress, because we both assess and document what students do by standards. The electronic scoring/grading system allows us, at parent/teacher conferences, to pull up any or all of the assignments or standards taught, display the student's score, show where the student is headed, and explain exactly where that student needs continued practice.

Teachers in co-teaching situations have the benefit of another set of eyes and another person's judgment regarding student performance. Synchronizing assessment and instruction leads to more meaningful and effective collaboration that not only advances specific student performance but also increases and improves overall communication.

✦ Time to Reflect ✦

How do you think "clipboard" monitoring and electronic scoring would benefit you and your students with special needs?

Using GANAG to Mind the Gap in the Resource Classroom

A new class session was just underway, and Ryan Finley stood before his nine students and smiled. As he observed, they filled out their "tickets"—objective score sheets—and then put their pencils down. Now that he was GANAGing his lesson, his 5th grade students knew the routine. As Ryan proceeded to guide them through the instruction, they took notes, worked in pairs, and asked questions. At the end of the lesson, they self-assessed and turned in completed objective score sheets. The class ran like a Swiss watch.

Ryan teaches students with severe emotional and behavioral difficulties. He and many of his colleagues in the special education department focus every day on attending to the needs of their pupils and the related demands of scheduling and managing caseloads. He indicated to us that he had never really used a lesson planning schema before, as his days and his students were unpredictable. His focus was whether or not his students could "make it"—first, in the regular classrooms and, eventually, in their lives beyond school. He says he had not always been able to focus on academics due to student misbehavior.

Like many other teachers we have worked with, Ryan's thinking about the concept of minding the gap sparked lots of follow-up questions. He admits that when he first heard about GANAG and was told, "This is how you will be planning lessons this year," he rolled his eyes at "yet another 'in' thing for us to do." As Ryan shared with us a little more about his instructional situation, he asked questions about GANAG and the resource classroom:

1. Can I GANAG a lesson for students with different IEP goals who are working at different grade levels?

2. Can my students be expected to interact with the goals?

3. Should I let the students get feedback from each other?

4. What should I do if there is another teacher working with me? How do we both GANAG?

Even as Ryan started asking the questions (instead of insisting that his students could not do those things), he began to answer them. Using a blank GANAG template, he wrote out an English lesson about the literary technique of personification. As we talked about the stages in GANAG and the strategies Ryan's students might use as they worked through the lesson, Ryan began to realize if he was going to manage instruction more deliberately, he would need to manage time and classroom behavior differently, too—and better.

Before long, Ryan became a self-proclaimed "GANAGophile," planning all of his lessons to incorporate each of the GANAG stages, sharing his adaptations with cooperating teachers, and even asking some of the other support teachers in his school to observe and score his students on the objectives when they were in his class. Ryan and these teachers walked around with clipboards, recording student progress on the curriculum objectives—the first time this kind of objective-based record keeping had been deliberately done for special education students. Soon, he said, it became the new normal.

Among the surprises for Ryan was that the GANAG schema became very automatic for him and for his students. The flow of the lessons kept them in sync with each other. The behavioral outbursts seemed reduced, and he now believes that he is more cognizant of the students' academic progress as well as their behavioral progress.

> I have experienced such positive encounters with my students as I continue to tweak and fine-tune lessons utilizing the GANAG model. When we state our goals, verbally and in writing, then discuss prior knowledge, rating our own understanding of the new information, the students really seem to grasp the concepts at a deeper level.

When a teacher as well respected as Ryan Finley becomes the positive deviant, others follow. When other teachers realized that he was finding one success after another with his students, they were much more open to the idea of making pedagogical changes rather than searching for excuses. As Ryan shared his methods and success with cooperating teachers, they came on board, and their skepticism toward lesson planning with GANAG turned into open-mindedness and even enthusiasm.

Now, let's take a second look at the questions Ryan posed about using GANAG in a pull-out special education environment. They are questions we frequently hear from special educators and are deserving of clear and specific answers.

1. *Can I GANAG a lesson for students with different IEP goals who are working at different grade levels?*

Yes. Whether working in a designated special education class or in an inclusion class, IEP goals, in tandem with designated grade-level curriculum goals, serve as the first "G" of GANAG and the student self-assessment that is the foundation for last "G." These goals bookend a lesson and involve students seeing and participating in their own progress. Just as teachers who work with English language learners use language goals and also curriculum goals for students at all levels of language proficiency, special education teachers can use

IEP goals and appropriate curriculum goals to help students with differing IEP expectations at any grade level.

2. *Can my students be expected to interact with the goals?*

Yes. Ryan found that his special education students became much more likely to participate in their learning once they knew what their learning goals were and were taught how to assess their own progress. GANAG offers a "place" for active learning to occur. Predictable routines and a feeling of control over their own learning are essential to engaging special education students. Allowing them to interact with their goals by seeking feedback, asking questions, and monitoring their own progress gives them a level of participation and autonomy that helps to diminish behavior problems and accelerate learning.

3. *Should I let students with special needs get feedback from other special needs students?*

Yes. If a teacher provides clear curriculum goals for all students in the special education or inclusion classroom, students can learn to seek feedback from and give feedback to one another. Students have a great deal to learn from their classmates. Short cooperative learning sessions allow teachers to monitor how and how well students are using peer feedback to pursue learning goals so that they can provide redirection, as needed. Again, GANAG facilitates these efforts.

4. *What should I do if I am working with another teacher? How do we both GANAG?*

As discussed previously, GANAGPlus is specifically designed for these situations. Co-teaching models, synchronized with GANAG, show how educators working in inclusion classes can make the GANAGPlus process work smoothly and allow each of them to teach and assess in ways that exponentially strengthen their teaching practices and students' learning gains. GANAGPlus explicitly shows how the incorporation of these models and the nine high-yield strategies into the GANAG schema works to increase achievement for special education students.

Complicated Questions, Simple Answers

Ryan's success in special education reminds us of a quotation attributed to Dr. Seuss: "Sometimes the questions are complicated and the answers are simple." Teachers can begin to change the tide regarding the frustration about educating special needs students when empowered with the right tool. We are convinced that what they need is a daily lesson planning tool—GANAG or GANAGPlus—that incorporates research-based strategies and a compelling communication device to describe students' successes in terms of seeing anticipated results. Simple practices, such as using student self-assessment objective score sheets and teacher tracking forms, maximize feedback and increase engagement in every classroom.

Minding the achievement gap one classroom at a time means shifting improvement efforts from the school to the classroom, and it requires special education teachers to join with their colleagues in changing automatic teaching habits when preparing and delivering lessons. Special educators can sharpen their pedagogical saws in the same way that general education teachers do, collaborating together to improve learning for all children.

Educator Voice

Mark Bazata, High School English Teacher and Co-Teacher

When Wisconsin teacher Mark Bazata began co-teaching his high school English class, he hoped the experience would better equip him to help all of his students succeed. Making the transition to two teachers in the classroom became easier when Mark received training in the co-teaching models and added the "Plus" to the GANAG lesson planning he was already doing.

From Skeptical to 100 Percent

A year after I started using GANAG, my school administrators informed me that I would be co-teaching two of my English 2 classes. I had seen special education teachers in my school, but other than a few e-mails and an occasional "hi" in the hallways, I really didn't know them. I was concerned that planning and teaching with another teacher would hinder my ability to engage my students and create interesting lesson plans. I also worried that it might slow my productivity.

On the first day of training, I sat down with my co-teacher, Sherry Zwicky, feeling like I was entering into an arranged marriage. We started with the typical chitchat, but things quickly became serious as we discussed discipline philosophies, grading practices, and classroom procedures. Eventually, we discussed lesson planning. I explained that I had been using the GANAG method.

"Great!" Sherry said, "I've been doing the same thing." We both laughed, and the tension eased. Since we were co-teaching, we decided to use GANAGPlus.

I discovered that planning with Sherry was easier than I had expected, and I was surprised to find that co-teaching actually made me more productive. From the beginning, it was important to us that our students would view both of us as equals, not as one teacher and one "helper." GANAGPlus guided us to be intentional about using different co-teaching models and consistent with our lesson plans. If we started seeing a pattern of "one teach, one assist," we would deliberately change it in the next lesson.

Because Sherry was new to teaching an English curriculum that I had been teaching for 10 years, I had to avoid just doing what I had always done. For Sherry to have ownership in the class, she needed to have as much responsibility for planning as I did. In some cases, that meant modifying existing lessons; in other cases, we had to create lessons from scratch. This was invigorating. Sherry brought innovative ideas that I never would have thought of trying.

Although Sherry and I had common planning time for creating lessons, we also needed to find a way to share lesson plans with other people: English language teaching staff, paraprofessionals, and other specialists who also were co-teaching English 2. We had a large group of professionals involved with our students, and there had to be a way for all of us to communicate. We were able to create a simple distribution list using my e-mail so that when I sent new GANAGPlus lesson plans to Sherry, I copied them to everyone else. With very little extra work on my part, a large group of people could access our teaching plans, including our co-teaching models and the curriculum we were teaching in lessons.

I once heard that in a marriage, if both people only give 50 percent, they will end up with only 25 percent of a marriage; it takes 100 percent from both people to make a 100 percent marriage. Co-teaching is no different. From the beginning, Sherry and I each made a commitment to be responsible for all of our students. Instead of Sherry helping only the students with special needs, we would exchange roles, so that I sometimes would help students who needed assistance while Sherry would take responsibility for the rest of the class.

"Less Defined Teacher Roles" Equals "More Unified Student Roles"

Over the course of the school year, our co-teaching roles became less defined. If some students needed extra help with an essay, for example, I could pull them out of class and hold writing conferences with them. When we had students who needed help taking tests, Sherry would take them to another room to read their tests to them. With GANAGPlus providing a structural safety net, it was possible for us to cease being "a special education teacher" and "a general education" teacher, and we became two teachers who taught according to our strengths rather than our set roles. As our role distinctions faded, we found that student "labels" also became less and less important. By the middle of the year, Sherry and I began making modifications for students who needed it, even though they had no identified disability. We knew that they still had to show proficiency on the unit standards, and GANAGPlus always kept the goals as paramount at the beginning, middle, and end of every lesson. If students needed help, we helped them, whether they had an IEP or not.

Since modifications, accommodations, and IEP goals became a part of all the lessons Sherry and I planned together, I've found myself using them to help students with disabilities in my other classes. For example, I now have learning targets that make it clear that every student is required to show proficiency in certain skills, even with modifications and accommodations.

Co-Teaching Brought Success Within and Beyond the Co-Taught Classroom

Over the past few years, as our school continued the practice of co-teaching in inclusion classrooms, the student failure rate has dropped dramatically from 20 percent to just a handful of chronically truant students. Reading scores on our state tests have increased by double digits. The achievement gap for students with disabilities has been cut in half. Students have made incredible gains in their language arts skills, especially in our co-taught classes. Problems with grade inflation have faded.

Among other changes, students in our school are no longer permitted to turn in extra-credit work to improve lackluster scores. Grades now reflect students' actual skill levels, not simply their ability to turn in worksheets. Students who previously fell through the cracks because they weren't labeled with a disability receive the help they need to succeed. Honor students work harder to hone their skills through regular class assignments rather than on extra-credit assignments. Students with disabilities who feared they would never pass English class have found that with a little bit of work, they can actually do well in class.

Having embraced the experience of working with a co-teacher, using the lesson planning tools to stay focused on student-centered goals, and realizing all these gains, it strikes me now, after 10 years of teaching, that the most important factor influencing student success in my classroom really is me.

Afterword

PARKER J. PALMER (2007) CALLS IT "THE COURAGE TO TEACH" inward decision a teacher can make to live "divided no more" (p. 16(intriguing concept is Palmer's way of explaining that individual teach and do have an extraordinary impact on student learning when they dec to criticize the educational institution but rather to examine their own t practices and actions with the intent of improving student learning.

We meet many teachers every week who care deeply about learning and are interested in ideas and strategies for raising achiev During our conversation, inevitably the discussion moves toward reasc schools work for *some* students but not for others. Sometimes those are budget related, connected to the history of past initiatives, or li leadership. Sometimes the reasons have to do with the individual ch his or her personal conditions.

When a teacher "minds the gap" for students whose achievem been marginalized by resources, language, or disabilities, that teacher is a courageous decision to let go of excuses, shake off complacency, embr reflection, and take deliberate action, leveraging research and sound ins to help students achieve the learning gains they need and deserve. It h our pleasure to share the experiences and perspectives of many such throughout this book. When Jill Cullis realized that she was the only c could change her teaching, she did, and her students have benefitted f changes she made in her classroom. Ileana Davis decided to change l taught English language learners after realizing that she had done everything she could up to that point and that it was time to find a new approach that would help translate her efforts into better student learning. Ryan Finley realized that he could change his mind about teaching students with special needs by focusing on how he planned to teach and then deliver high-yield lessons. These teachers, the many contributors you've heard from in this book, and countless others we work with in the field have claimed what Palmer calls the "identity and integrity from which good living, as well as good teaching, comes" (2007, p. 167). In short, a teacher who minds the gap is demonstrating the belief that that every student can learn, and every student can achieve.

Living undivided as teachers means going beyond what can be valid criticism of the school as an organization, the taxpayers and funding sources, our students' parents, and other factors beyond our immediate control. It means embracing the power and knowledge we have; it means changing what we can change, even when that is not easy. Teachers live undivided when they communicate learning intentions, teach to those goals, and create an environment in the classroom that provides students with the frequent feedback that leads to better achievement. With the time they have and the resources available— objective score sheets, interactive notebooks, curriculum documents, a plan book, a grade book—they go about improving student learning one classroom at a time.

Acknowledgments

Our thanks to the following "positive deviant" teachers, specialists, and administrators:

Mark Bazata, Kevin Broznik, Gale Cameron, Jill Cullis, Missy Daniels, Ileana Davis, Rebecca Day, Alex DeMatteis, Karen DuChene, Ryan Finley, Sue Furcinito, Mat Gover, Patty Grossman, Kathy Gwidt, Pat Hamilton, Melanie Hansen, Vicki Haverland, Jennie Hensgen, Ron Hensley, Susan Hensley, Ray Highway, Joanele Hoce, Julie Housaman, Lena Joch, Jill Jones, Stephanie Lane, Tammy Lang, Linda Law, Gretchen Lee, Ginny McElhaney, Chris Meyers, Linda Mishkin, Gary Nunnally, Dana Paykos, Judy Pottle, Diane Quirk, Tammy Riedel, Lisa Setsor, Trent Scott, Jenn Sykora, Brad Tate, Vanessa Trujillo-Smith, Laura Turner, Dan Young, and Sherry Zwicky.

We would also like to thank the staff at ASCD. Katie Martin has worked tirelessly on our books to ensure the right voice, clarity, and balance. And thanks to Laura Lawson, Genny Ostertag, and Scott Willis for their support throughout the publishing process.

References and Resources

Arkansas Department of Education. (2010). *Arkansas curriculum frameworks.* Available: http://www. arkansased.org/educators/curriculum/frameworks.html

Civic Enterprises & Peter Hart Research Associates for the Bill & Melinda Gates Foundation. (2006). *The silent epidemic: Perspectives of high school dropouts.* Washington, DC: Bridgeland, Dilulio, & Morison.

Cody, A. (2009, August 19). Living in dialogue: California scores rise, but gap remains [blog post]. *Education Week Teacher Online.* Retrieved August 4, 2011, from http://blogs.edweek.org/teachers/ living-in-dialogue/2009/08/california_scores_rise_but_gap.html

Common Core Curriculum Mapping Project [website]. Available: http://www.commoncore.org

Common Core State Standards Initiative [website]. Available: http://www.corestandards.org

Council for Exceptional Children [website]. Available: http://www.cec.sped.org

Covey, S. (1989). *The 7 habits of highly successful people.* New York: Simon and Schuster.

Echevarria, J. (2006). Helping English language learners succeed. *Principal Leadership, 6*(6), 16–21.

Echevarria, J., Vogt, M. E., & Short, D. (2004). *Making content comprehensible for English language learners: The SIOP Model* (2nd ed.). Boston: Allyn & Bacon.

Edmonds, R. (1979, October). Effective schools for the urban poor. *Educational Leadership 37*(1), 22.

Ferguson, R. (2008). *Toward excellence with equity: An emerging vision for closing the achievement gap.* Cambridge, MA: Harvard Education Press.

Forum for Education and Democracy. (2008). *Democracy at risk: The need for a new federal policy in education.* Washington, DC: Forum for Education and Democracy.

Friend, M., & Hurley-Chamberlain, D. (n.d.). *Is co-teaching effective?* Retrieved August 4, 2011, from http://www.cec.sped.org/AM/Template.cfm?Section=Home&TEMPLATE=/CM/Content Display.cfm&CONTENTID=7504&CAT=none

Fu, D. (2004). Teaching ELL students in regular classrooms at the secondary level. *Voices from the Middle, 11*(4), 8–15.

Gersten, R., & Baker, S. (2000). What we know about effective instructional practices for English-language learners. *Exceptional Children, 66*(4), 454–470.

Glass, G. V. (2008). *Fertilizers, pills, and magnetic strips: The fate of public education in America.* Charlotte, NC: Information Age Publishing.

Guskey, T. R., & Bailey, J. M. (2000). *Developing grading and reporting systems for student learning.* Thousand Oaks, CA: Corwin.

Harper, C., & de Jong, E. (2004). Misconceptions about teaching English-language learners. *Journal of Adolescent and Adult Literacy, 48*(2), 152–162.

Hattie, J. (2009). *Visible learning: A synthesis of over 800 meta-analyses relating to achievement.* London: Routledge.

Hill, J., & Flynn, K. (2006). *Classroom instruction that works with English language learners.* Alexandria, VA: ASCD.

Hunter, M. (1982). *Mastery teaching.* Thousand Oaks, CA: Corwin.

Johnson, S. (2008). *The invention of air.* New York: Riverside Books.

Kirshenbaum, H., Napier, R., & Simon, S. B. (1971).*Wad-ja-get? The grading game in American education.* New York: Hart.

Marzano, R. J. (2000). *Transforming grading.* Alexandria, VA: ASCD.

Marzano, R. J., Pickering, D. J., & Pollock, J. E. (2001). *Classroom instruction that works: Research-based strategies for increasing student achievement.* Alexandria, VA: ASCD.

Mathews, J. (2009, August 17). Age-old problem, perpetually absent solution: Fitting special education to students' needs. *Washington Post.* Retrieved August 4, 2011, from http://www.washingtonpost.com/wp-dyn/content/article/2009/08/16/AR2009081601805.html

Organisation for Economic Co-operation and Development (OECD). (2011). *Education at a glance: OECD indicators.* Paris: OECD Publishing.

Palmer, P. J. (2007). *The courage to teach: Exploring the inner landscape of a teacher's life* (10th anniversary ed.). San Francisco: Jossey-Bass.

Pascale, R., Sternin, J., & Sternin, M. (2010). *The power of positive deviance: How unlikely innovators solve the world's toughest problems.* Cambridge, MA: Harvard Business Press.

Payne, R. (2005). *A framework for understanding poverty.* Highlands, TX: aha! Process.

Pollock, J. E. (2007). *Improving student learning one teacher at a time.* Alexandria, VA: ASCD.

Pollock, J. E. (2012). *Feedback: The hinge that joins teaching and learning.* Thousand Oaks, CA: Corwin.

Pollock, J. E., & Ford, S. M. (2009). *Improving student learning one principal at a time.* Alexandria, VA: ASCD.

Pressley, M, Gaskins, I. W., Solic, K., & Collins, S. (2006). A portrait of Benchmark School: How a school produces high achievement in students who previously failed. *Journal of Educational Psychology, 98*(2), 282–306.

Rothstein, R. (1998). *The way we were? The myths and realities of America's student achievement.* New York: Century Foundation Press.

State of Washington, Office of Superintendent of Public Instruction. (n.d.). English Language Development Standards. Retrieved December 3, 2011, from http://www.k12.wa.us/migrant bilingual/eld.aspx

Stigler, J. W., & Hiebert, J. (1998). Teaching is a cultural activity. *American Education, 22*(4). Available: http://www.aft.org/pdfs/americaneducator/winter1998/TeachingWinter98.pdf

Strong American Schools. (2008, April). *A stagnant nation: Why American students are still at risk.* Washington, DC: Author. Available: http://broadeducation.org/asset/1128-a%20stagnant%20 nation.pdf

World-Class Instructional Design and Assessment. (2011). *WIDA's Can-Do descriptors by grade-level cluster.* Retrieved August 4, 2011, from http://www.wida.us/standards/CAN_DOs/index.aspx

Index

The letter *f* following a page number denotes a figure. GANAG steps are shown in all CAPS.

About the Authors

Jane E. Pollock, PhD, is the director of Learning Horizon, Inc. A former English as a Second Language teacher, general classroom teacher, and school administrator, she consults long-term with schools worldwide to improve student learning, instructional practices, and supervision. She is the author of *Improving Student Learning One Teacher at a Time* (2007) and *Feedback: The Hinge That Joins Teaching and Learning* (2012) and the coauthor of *Dimensions of Learning Teacher and Training Manuals* (1996); *Assessment, Grading and Record Keeping* (1999); *Classroom Instruction That Works* (2001); and *Improving Student Learning One Principal at a Time* (2009). She is a faculty member for ASCD. A native of Caracas, Venezuela, Janie earned degrees at the University of Colorado and Duke University. She can be reached at learninghorizon@msn.com or through her website, www.improvestudentlearning.com.

Sharon M. Ford, EdD, is a former special education and general classroom teacher with experience working with colleagues to develop IEP goals and help students achieve them. She most recently served as an assistant professor in the department of Administrative Leadership and Policy Studies in the Graduate School of Education at the University of Colorado at Denver, where the primary focus of her work was school leadership to promote the professional development of K–12 teachers in all kinds of classrooms, including inclusion and resource classrooms. Sharon has also worked in a state department of education, supervising mentor teachers in numerous school and classroom settings. She has also advised doctoral and master's degree students and taught courses for graduate students seeking licenses as school principals and superintendents. Sharon's work has been published in refereed journals, including the *Journal of School Leadership,* and she is the co-author, with Jane E. Pollock, of *Improving Student Learning One Principal at a Time.* She is the regional representative for a seven-state area to the Professors of Secondary School Administration, National Association of Secondary School Principals, and is president of the Colorado Association of Professors of School Administration. Sharon earned degrees at the University of Colorado and at Whittier College in California. She can be reached at sharonf3@me.com.

Margaret (Peggy) M. Black is the director of the Center for Diverse Student Learning. Concentrating on the areas of integrating service delivery models with an emphasis on English language learner programs, Peggy works with schools to increase the efficiency of program development for sustained growth in student learning. Influencing effective teaching for the 21st century is the core of her consulting and professional development work. Before assuming her current post, Peggy was a director in a regional service agency, a policy advisor to the Wisconsin governor's office, a school board president, and a classroom teacher. She is an adjunct faculty member at various universities. Peggy earned degrees at the University of Wisconsin–Madison and National Louis University. She can be reached at margaretblack.wi@gmail.com.

Related ASCD Resources

At the time of publication, the following ASCD resources were available (ASCD stock numbers appear in parentheses). For up-to-date information about ASCD resources, go to www.ascd.org. You can search the complete archives of *Educational Leadership* at http://www.ascd.org/el.

ASCD Edge

Exchange ideas and connect with other educators interested in closing the achievement gap, assessment and grading, enhancing professional practice, teaching English language learners, and inspiring student motivation on the social networking site ASCD Edge™ at http://ascdedge.ascd.org/

Print Products

Changing the Way You Teach, Improving the Way Students Learn by Giselle O. Martin-Kniep and Joanne Picone-Zocchia (#108001)

Classroom Instruction That Works: Research-Based Strategies for Increasing Student Achievement, 2nd edition by Ceri B. Dean, BJ Stone, Elizabeth Hubbell, and Howard Pitler (#111001)

Creating the Opportunity to Learn: Moving from Research to Practice to Close the Achievement Gap by Wade Boykin and Pedro Noguera (#107016)

Enhancing Student Achievement: A Framework for School Improvement by Charlotte F. Danielson (#102109)

Improving Student Learning One Teacher at a Time by Jane E. Pollock (#107005)

Videos and Mixed Media

How to Use Interactive Notebooks (#606058)

Raising the Literacy Achievement of English Language Learners DVD and Facilitator's Guide (#606122)

The Sights and Sounds of Equitable Practices DVD with Edwin Lou Javius (#610013)

Teaching Students with Learning Disabilities in the Regular Classroom DVD and Online Facilitator's Guide (#602084)

Online Courses

Achievement Gaps: An Introduction (#PD9OC63)

Content-Based Instruction for English Language Learners, 2nd Edition (#PD11OC120)

Inclusion: Implementing Strategies, 2nd Edition (#PD11OC122)

For more information: send e-mail to member@ascd.org; call 1-800-933-2723 or 703-578-9600, press 2; send a fax to 703-575-5400; or write to Information Services, ASCD, 1703 N. Beauregard St., Alexandria, VA 22311-1714 USA.